SELF-LOVE

A WOMAN'S BOOK OF
HEALING AND INSPIRATION

CHRISTINA FIOR

DISCLAIMER

The contents of this book are solely the opinion of the author and are not intended to be a substitute for medical or psychological advice by a licensed professional. The author and publisher advise readers to do their own research and consult their health care provider regarding their health and well-being.

SELF-LOVE
A Woman's Book of Healing and Inspiration
Authored by: Christina Fior

ISBN: 9781796468632

Printed in the United States

IN CELEBRATION

I celebrate all women whose
time has come to boldly become
all you are meant to be.

IN APPRECIATION

Thank you, Elizabeth England, for your brilliant
editorial contribution to this book

I extend my deepest appreciation to all of the teachers
and mentors in my life who have, by their example,
shown me a higher way.

SELF-LOVE

A WOMAN'S BOOK OF INSPIRATION

CONTENTS

9

INTRODUCTION

A UNIVERSAL STORY...

13

CHAPTER ONE

HEALING THE BROKEN HEART

25

CHAPTER TWO

SHAPE-SHIFTING OUR BELIEFS

41

CHAPTER THREE

REWARDING THE HEROINE

55

CHAPTER FOUR

RECLAIMING OUR BIRTHRIGHT

67

CHAPTER FIVE

LEARNING FROM SEASONED,
EMPOWERED WOMEN

83
CHAPTER SIX

CREATING A NEW FOUNDATION

93
CHAPTER SEVEN

SELF-REFERRED LOVE

107
CHAPTER EIGHT

EMBODYING THE EMPOWERED PATH

117
CHAPTER NINE

BECOMING CHANGE AGENTS

125
APPENDIX

KEY CONCEPTS OF EACH CHAPTER

133
RESOURCES

REFERENCES AND RECOMMENDATIONS

SELF-LOVE
A WOMAN'S BOOK OF INSPIRATION

INTRODUCTION

A UNIVERSAL STORY...

An inner revolution is on the rise. As women, it's our time to embody a deep appreciation for the depth and breadth of our life experiences. We have been weathered by life's storms, and although there may appear to be all manner of evidence to the contrary, we are on the cusp of a new horizon for our lives.

Our feminine journey commands respect as we continue to find our deeper purpose amidst the rigors of living in a predominantly masculine culture. We have seen the constructs of male domination being deconstructed before our eyes through the "Me Too" Movement. As empowered women, we're now compelled to bring balance to this equation and advance a new culture of love that has been long cocooning just beyond the veil.

The universal woman within is urging us to embody a grander idea of ourselves. As standard-bearers of a new global culture, we are compelled to give rise to the feminine principle within all mankind, restoring peace to the soul of humanity.

The old-world order is swiftly crumbling beneath our feet as the folly of war, abuse of resources, financial greed and competition are gradually giving way to a new international community, to global sustainability, enlightened commerce and conscious collaboration.

This new world is giving birth to a feminine power that will no longer be denied as its healing force moves with fervor to restore hope to a world in peril.

As the discomfort of this global metamorphosis is taking place, many women are seeking to overcome their ancient suffering from victimization and low self-esteem, and regain their divine inheritance as wise, contemporary goddesses. Even those of us who have become successful business women, spiritual explorers, cultural creatives and/or devoted homemakers may be carrying lifetimes of guilt, shame, self-condemnation and fear in our DNA, not knowing how to completely set ourselves free.

As we begin to discover and employ the keys that unlock this shadow world, we can bring it to the light, and begin remodeling our interior world with the power of renewed self-love.

I invite you to be patient with the process.

The first three chapters of this book offer a deep exploration of a woman's voyage from entering into a human incarnation, followed by a series of dynamics commonly experienced at one time or another that have led us down the rabbit hole of love deprivation.

As a young child, I myself experienced sexual violation by my male peers. I also felt a mockery of my sexual innocence from puberty into my teens by older kids in my neighborhood. These humiliations initiated a paralyzing shock within me. An agonizing spiral of isolation and inadequacy began to spin its web as a core wound.

I had no outlet for sharing what I was experiencing so I became depressed and discouraged, two stereotyped flaws associated with females. The irony is, this form of mass stereotyping has continually imposed upon the soul of women, a denial of her feminine expression. Often women will sweep under the rug, the instigator of this insidious belief spiral. What is the instigator? This is the mystery to uncover and transform as we progress through these pages.

In continuing the formative years of my life, my primal beauty, feminine power and inherent wisdom became the subject of control before I had the discernment or the voice to stand for my truth. An agonizing feeling of loneliness sent me deep within myself as I became highly philosophical about life. I became aware of my empathic and intuitive gifts very early on—an inherently female skill that was not celebrated in the conservative, patriarchal society of the 1960s.

Like many budding beauties of the world, my innate brilliance as a woman became threatening to mediocre minds and my innocent feminine expressions were misunderstood and taken advantage of. I began to think something was wrong with me. So, I found myself in situations where I constantly edited my behavior in order to protect myself or appease others who were perpetrating the popular culture of that time period.

Over the years as I evolved, I became aware of how common this and other violations of our collective female innocence are.

During my decades as an intuitive counselor and transformation coach, I've heard hundreds of accountings by women whose feminine essence was violated very early on in one form or another. Like me, they gradually lost the inner spark of believing in themselves and their purpose in life because the natural expression of their brilliance was labeled unimportant or self-absorbed.

So many of us then, have become preoccupied with serving others at the expense of our own well-being and continued self-discovery. Over the years we've coped, as we've resigned ourselves to a disempowering idea of self-love, incrementally invalidating our core knowing. This ancient suffering within the soul of woman, in one form or another, has also been passed on in our DNA from generation to generation, compounding the depth of these experiences.

As a reflection of my own life sojourn, I'm privileged to share with you a fascinating discovery of some empowering, universal principles. I have observed that, while individually our arduous paths are unique and personal; there are so many more commonalities of the heart and soul that we, as women, share.

This is our golden moment then to unleash our feminine genius and rekindle our innermost dreams, infused with renewed courage and creativity. It begins by developing compassion for the bumpy journey we have endured. We have been through the fire. We've been seasoned. We're now becoming delicious and spicy self-empowered women.

CHAPTER ONE
HEALING THE BROKEN HEART

A woman is like a tea bag –
you never know how strong she is
until she gets in hot water.

—Eleanor Roosevelt

CHAPTER ONE
HEALING THE BROKEN HEART

It takes guts to become a self-empowered woman.

It takes audacity to carve out one's path and become impervious to the thoughts, opinions and expectations of others. It takes courage to prevail over the shock and trauma of our life experiences, and the subsequent beliefs we may have accumulated about ourselves of being unworthy…or even incapable of love and lasting happiness.

Moreover, it takes extraordinary self-compassion to dispel the myth that we have to be long-suffering in order to achieve approval, fulfillment or success.

Inherently, each of us is a divine masterpiece, holding within us an exquisite original design of our full potential self. With our own unique colors, curves, brains and expressions, we are meant to shine and to inspire. But life has become so complicated! How did we get to this place?

Let's take a voyage, starting from the beginning. Perhaps we'll acquire new insights for reintegrating self-love into our lives and fueling the design of our ongoing journey with renewed passion and purpose.

The Soul's Voyage

There's a divine intelligence that works within each soul to determine its sequence of human incarnations. Let's imagine for a moment that our souls are in the stage of pre-conception. While there are souls who are content to maintain their journey in spiritual realms, each of us have labored to incarnate into a physical body in order to learn the lessons of earth and advance our soul's evolution.

During sex, up to 150 million sperm swim upstream toward a woman's fallopian tubes on their mission to fertilize an egg. Only a few hundred will even come close to the egg because of the natural barriers that exist within her body. So, as the choice sperm that penetrates the egg, our entry transforms the surface of the egg so that no other sperm can enter. At the moment of fertilization, our divine blueprint and our genetic makeup is complete.

The creation of our life unfolding within our mother's womb is a miracle and a mystery. The moment our soul triumphs as a new life force inside her liquid uterine cocoon, the alchemy of cell multiplication takes place. Like a microcosm of the universe, we contain within us, spiraling worlds of unlimited potential.

By seizing this opportunity through the sheer act of conception, we have each rightfully claimed our inherent self-worth to fulfill our sacred purpose.

Just as the vast galaxies give birth to new stellar bodies, our cells and the light of the mitochondria continue to multiply as an ecstatic dance forming us from within. Connected to the womb of creation we now become a microscopic bud attached to our mother through the umbilical cord. The pulsations of the life force within her begin to ignite our heart, then our tiny organs and body systems.

As we complete our pre-birth cycle, we're suddenly confronted by an immense pressure as we begin squeezing our way through a dense, narrow passageway. Our senses are feverishly fielding a range of imposing sensations like noise, light, temperature and a peculiar impression we call 'touch.' We extend out our shaky arms, and in our fragile effort to proclaim our identity we wail out our first primal cry, *I'm here! But, who am I?*

For many of us, we've found ourselves in complete embodiment shock and largely forgetful of our core identity and our prior sublime spiritual existence. Even amidst the most nurturing of environments, we cannot shield ourselves from the harsh welcome our budding souls encounter. We've entered a very dense platform of experience, and we're about to engage ourselves in a live theater of sorts, fraught with complicated rules of engagement.

As newborns, most of us are swaddled in the memory of love by the warmth of our mothers embrace. For others of us, we're swiftly disengaged from our biological connection and placed into the arms of a new maternal guardian. And sadly, some of us find ourselves unwelcomed or even blamed for being born.

Throughout the stages of our earth sojourn, we encounter a variety of human connections. Our lives are filled with experiences of kindness and resourcefulness by the human spirit while other times we're stunned and even traumatized by careless acts of inhumane behavior. Every event along our journey adds to our psyche's categorization of the way life is and what our experiences will be.

While many of us seek to maintain our original innocense where love was the governing force of all things, our earthly existence has been layered over with centuries of humankind's individual and collective misuse of the free agency we came in with.

Throughout the centuries, our global community has continuously engaged in warring and competition on multiple levels. These, along with the misuse of our technological advancements, sexual obsessions and financial greed have created within the collective soul, a sense of separation from our divine source. And sadly, too often there is an indifference to the ramifications it has created.

For many of us, we ache for the promise of paradise on Earth, yet we find ourselves on a lonely and unpopular path because we simply don't fit in with the stratification of society and its popularized standards. With all the distractions of modern day living, it's easy to forget that we came here to be co-creators with our source and reflect the brilliant divine mind present within us.

A New Generation of Hope

Paradoxically, there's a distinctive generation of individuals being born today who seem to embody a sense of clarity and pre-destiny. They are the wide-eyed souls who have primarily emerged from the pioneering parents of the Baby Boomer generation and subsequent Generation X. The Boomers and the Xers, otherwise known as the Indigo and Crystal Children, are the revolutionaries who have stood up against the norms of society and continue to forge new pathways towards liberation.

Perhaps knowingly or unknowingly, the Boomers and Xers, along with other revolutionaries throughout time have laid the foundation for others to be born in a more advanced evolutionary environment.

We're now experiencing the rise of Generation Y otherwise known as the Echo Boomers, followed by Generation Z, also known as the Connected Generation. The enlightened ones of these generations are also known as the Rainbow Children.

The end of the generation alphabet alludes to the idea that we are in the end times as we know it, and that the future is yet unscripted with endless potential. Many souls embodying today are consciously coming forward to redefine the human story and vastly advance our global community as a turning point in history.

The Challenge to Rise Above

Even with the advancements of the consciousness revolution, we together, still find ourselves in the arduous process of transforming the encrusted patterns of history along with the unique life lessons that accompany our personal embodiment. And we are now faced with new challenges brought on by greedy superpowers.

Our current life span may have become tainted over the years from experiencing confusion with the undependable nature of human behavior and perhaps at times, even being an instigator of it. Human undependability does not resonate with the natural order of love that was encoded upon our souls since the beginning of time. Therefore, conflict has ensued.

Those of us who have come from stable homes with loving parents may even find ourselves deeply wounded. Why? We may be carrying within our genetic memory, a series of wounds from our ancestral history along with the unresolved wounds brought in from former lifetimes.

Perhaps, this explains why some individuals who appear to 'have it all' find themselves on a path of self-destruction. They simply do not know how to identify what's ailing them deep within their core, nor have they developed the skills for liberating themselves from their internal anguish.

Even the most brilliant of souls can find themselves in a silent desperation, often resorting to anesthetizing themselves via self-medicating, overeating, over-sexing or self-loathing. The once shining light of the soul may subsequently spiral into the secrecy of the shadow self, losing touch with the frequency of their soul's inner broadcast and their refuge of peace that lies just beyond the veil.

Other souls who have been born through unwholesome parental upbringings may have long prepared themselves for the task of fulfilling their life purpose 'no matter what.' Their souls may have generated lifetimes of good will and therefore, the parents they we're born through were less relevant than the larger purpose they pre-destined for their lives. In this case, a parent's own evolution might be enhanced, simply by being associated with their child's advancements.

Peeling the Layers of the Onion

If you have ever peeled an onion, then you know that the first thin, papery layer reveals another thin, papery layer, and that layer reveals another, and another...and before you know it you have hundreds of layers all over the kitchen table and thousands of tears in your eyes, sorry that you ever started peeling in the first place, and wishing that you had left the onion alone to wither away on the shelf of the pantry while you went on with your life...even if that meant never again enjoying the complicated and overwhelming taste of this strange and bitter vegetable.

— Lemony Snicket

Unraveling the complicated layers of our life is like peeling the layers of an onion. We may assume that it's easier to leave the layers of our pain and suffering on the shelf and avoid our exposure to the potency of the unraveling process. Yet, by negating the tears of a buried journey, we may very well deny ourselves the delectable rediscovery of our core essence—that which seasons our life with a spicy richness and depth of meaning.

To bring relevance to this concept, let's return to our voyage now as a young, impressionable female soul progressing along into a maturing woman. Somewhere along the journey, we may have found ourselves becoming incrementally broken-hearted. This occurs, not so much as a result of a series of failed love relationships; they are often symptomatic of a deeper wound aching inside.

Some of us have become broken-hearted from having experienced a separation from our original innocence as we entered into a human body. With all of the distractions of daily living, especially in modern society, we've forgotten why we came. We may have been besieged by a set of traumas in our life—perhaps by experiencing parental discord, abandonment, neglect, abuse or even peer pressure.

Each of these assaults on our original innocence are severely wounding to the delicate budding psyche. It can dampen the spirit and intimidate us into becoming small. It can cause us to behave in an edited manner which is counterintuitive to our core knowing in order to defend ourselves, or to satisfy an agenda imposed by others for the sake of keeping peace.

These learned behaviors often occur at times when our young and impressionable souls have had no reference by which to protect our innocence or discern the difference between healthy and unhealthy behaviors. Thus, we may have created within us a self-sabotaging set of beliefs based on a skewed emotional norm. This acquired norm often becomes a comfort zone we defer ourselves to, which then sets the stage upon which we play out our lives and attract to us the actors within our personal life theater.

Many of us have learned then, how to negate our own inner sensibilities, resulting in becoming reactionary to life rather than emerging as self-made women who operate from an empowered, co-creative vantage point. Subconsciously, we may have convinced ourselves that all is well when in fact, step-by-step, we have become broken-hearted for being unseen and uncelebrated for who we truly are as well as the splendid, unique purpose of our lives.

Perhaps insomnia sometimes occurs from the pain of a woman's departure from herself, along with her anguish and fear that her life may never fulfill its sacred, passionate purpose. Many women, due to no fault of their own, have lost the plot of their own lives.

Who will understand this plight?

Until we, as women, begin to quiet the chatter of the outer world and communicate with our own soul, we may find that traditional counseling is but a band-aid to the problem. Our purpose here is to cultivate an environment within us that recognizes and roots out the beliefs (like weeds from a garden) that have taken us off course and caused us to live a victimized, self-deprecating life.

The Power of Positive Association

Life becomes magical as we learn to develop new emotional associations with our life experiences. Recalling our inherent self-worth as divine beings who have triumphed in becoming human beings is reason enough for fulfilling our destiny.

Given the outcome of embodiment shock and the arduous path of the human experience, self-compassion along the way gives us a new kind of strength to forge healthier pathways for our lives. The next phase of the journey requires us to shape-shift our elaborate and sometimes misdirected belief spiral, and incrementally recalibrating our course.

We are powerful and magnificent beyond belief. Once we are willing to grasp this idea, the alchemy of self-love truly begins.

SELF-LOVE RITUAL

Tuning in and Toning with Your Heart

Take time to create a personal sanctuary in your home. Carve out a special corner in your bedroom, a patio near a fountain, a den or wherever you can establish a place of peace.

Place flowers, pictures, talismans and other cherished mementos around you on a designated table, dresser or shelf to remind you of nature and the love that surrounds you. Consider this your altar, a sacred space where you meditate, reflect, affirm and co-create with the Source. It is your place of peace where you can 'alter' your life in profound ways.

Sit or stand, whichever is most comfortable. Allow your body to gently and naturally sway back and forth, or side-to-side. Place your hands over your heart and listen with compassion to what it is aching to be expressed.

Allow your heart to be heavy. Pay attention to your feelings without editing or judging yourself. Sound out these feelings and let the ache of your heart be heard. For instance, you may express, *I am lonely and unfulfilled. I feel unseen and uncelebrated for who I truly am.* Gently caress your heart as a means of self-comfort.

Gently touch other parts of your body that are holding tension and let them reveal to you, why they are in pain. Lovingly listen and give yourself time. Sound out the feelings. Express any messages your body is telling you. Take a few deep breaths, with an emphasis on the out breath. As you release the breath, shake out your body and sound out any residual feelings.

Next, as you calm yourself, allow your hands to fan out to each side as if to open your heart. Envision a giant pink waterfall washing over you, taking with it the anguish of heartbreak and all other burdens that have dampened your spirit. Allow this waterfall of light to increase, bathing your cells with renewal.

Sound out your sighs of relief. As you begin to feel cleansed, assure yourself and affirm in present time, positive qualities about yourself such as:

I am lovable and worthy of being deeply and unconditionally loved for who I truly am. I am grateful for my unique and important purpose in this world. Daily, I am fulfilling my hearts true calling.

Determine to affirm joy into your life, and into your body. Reclaim your worthiness and your birthright to be happy.

As you are expressing your innate wisdom, allow the intonation of your voice to open up to the organic expression of the timeless song of your heart. Sing with wild abandon! You may find your words will disappear as your heart begins toning and resonating its healing power throughout your body, mind and spirit.

Your mind's engagement with your emotional world is extremely magnetic. Imagine what it would 'feel' like to have the qualities you desire for your life right now. Give yourself permission to accept it. When repeated daily, this practice will build momentum to draw to you, the desired present time blessings.

You can use this exercise for any situation such as heartbreak over the loss of a loved one, feelings of betrayal, frustration or even self-destructive thoughts. It is also a powerful catalyst for moving forward unfulfilled desires that can no longer be denied.

CHAPTER TWO
SHAPE-SHIFTING
OUR BELIEFS

*Everything that happens to you is a
reflection of what you believe about yourself.
We cannot outperform our level of self-esteem.
We cannot draw to ourselves, more than
we 'think' we are worth.*

—*Iyanla Vanzant*

CHAPTER TWO
SHAPE-SHIFTING OUR BELIEFS

In order for us to shape-shift our beliefs and associated emotions, we must identify the core wounds we've accumulated during the early stages of our lives. Our belief systems, from the moment we are born, are acquired by our experiences and the choices we make within the realm of those experiences.

Our beliefs and their associated emotions become layered which stack up, one over the other, like an onion. At the center, holding all of these beliefs together, lays one or two core beliefs that have launched our belief spiral. If we've embodied a set of healthy beliefs and behaviors, they are likely rooted from positive experiences that took place early in life when our budding psyche was taking in information. We were literally in 'formation' of our pending reality.

On the contrary, if our young, impressionable psyche was surrounded by negative information in conflict with our innate innocence, we may have become wounded to the core. Over the course of years, these core wounds may have become so shrouded by the layers of our subconscious mind, they may seem inaccessible to identify and heal in present time.

If you or I were told, for instance, that we were born a 'mistake' by our parents and were subsequently treated as such, we may have developed a core belief that we are an imposition to life. We may have attracted circumstances that instigate self-sabotaging behaviors and relationships that verify the belief that we are undeserving of being valued and loved.

Year after year, we might find ourselves living in an unwholesome comfort zone; of either giving up or over-achieving due to feelings of unworthiness to be brilliant, productive and loveable. We may have lost touch with love's embrace and have long forgotten the original grand design of our lives that is still well within our reach.

Liberating Our Wounds

As we celebrate women who have become fully empowered feminine role models, in our hearts we intrinsically feel the pain of women grieving all over the world. Many of us have been mourning the loss of loved ones, the loss of our innocence, the loss of our feminine power and the missed opportunities along the way. The good news is, our wounded selves are on the threshold of massive transformation and ultimate liberation!

Discovering our core wounds is an inside job that requires kindhearted self-inquiry. Getting in touch with our internal damage can often evoke feelings of guilt, shame, and self-condemnation. When this occurs, we must realize that we're getting somewhere! This is a moment when we can become aware of the vibrations we've been carrying around, perhaps for our entire lives, or even in former lives—not knowing the keys for loving ourselves free.

It's time to listen and respond from within. Silent contemplation followed by sounding out the pain we're feeling inside (as described in Chapter One's Self-Love Ritual) are great catalysts for getting in touch with the hidden core wounds experienced at the early stages of life that have continued to run our show as adults. The act of contemplation bridges our outer awareness with our inner terrain. By sounding out the repressed emotions, we can release them from our cellular holding patterns, thus allowing us to externalize the pain associated with our layered wounds.

These wounds often begin to reveal themselves to us through mental and emotional self-talk that arise during the self-inquiry process such as: *I'm damaged goods;* or *anything bad that happens is my fault;* or *God has abandoned me.*

Having forgotten how truly powerful we are, we may have assumed these beliefs as our life laws. Unconsciously, we may have employed an emotionally-charged agreement with these beliefs and subsequent behaviors within our cells, thus becoming sorcerers of the worst kind upon our own soul.

We may have forgotten that we contain within us, the capacity to positively renew our cellular beliefs with a higher level of mindfulness. Knowing that our conscious, quantum universe continually reflects and refracts what we give our power to on multiple levels, we can literally "catch ourselves in the act" when unwholesome patterns arise, and course-correct with positive affirmative behaviors. As we do so, we attain a stronger internal compass by which to steer the course of our lives.

We Are Fluid Beings

This planet is being peopled by superior creatures who are going to save us, but they aren't arriving from the outside; they're arriving from the inside. They're bleeping in and out. They're our future selves coming back to pick us up, in order there might be a future.
                                            —*Marianne Williamson*

One of the most interesting phenomena our world's population is caught in, is 'static' behavior that often stems from indifference. We've forgotten what it's like to live as fluid beings who allow the tides of emotions within us to rise and fall.

It's natural for all of life on Earth to dance with the cycles and gravitational pull of the moon, sun and planets. Rather than deny our emotions and our passions, we can learn to employ effective ways for embracing them in order to enhance self-realization and communication with others. We can then begin transforming these emotions into powerful acts of co-creation with God as divine currency, leading to a more fluid and abundant life.

Our Emotions as Divine Currency

Consider for a moment, that your emotions (positive or negative) contain a power so great as to attract to you, the result of your emotionally charged beliefs. I like to refer to this as divine currency. Divine currency is a neutral force we are born with. This currency is tempered in our lives by our beliefs and the type of emotional associations we attach to our beliefs.

This explains why emotional release work is so effective.

The water content within each of us serves as an internal record keeper—a magnetic field of our emotionally charged beliefs. As we transform our beliefs, we change the vibration of the water in our cells which holds the resonance and the attraction principle of that belief within our electromagnetic field.

Personally, I love to release my pent-up emotions while walking alone on the beach. I literally shout out my truths and my emotions (and engage my body in the process) as I jump and dance to the ocean's timeless waves. The waves continuously lap up against the shore and remind me of the continuum of life beyond my moments of being stuck. This ocean ritual provides for me, a magical recharge of my divine currency by helping me release and transform my emotions and affirm my self-respect.

Another benefit of expressing our emotions while barefoot at the beach or in a lush nature-infused setting is that our internal circuitry becomes recalibrated by the power of earth's electromagnetic field. Our bodies become grounded and infused with negative ions which in turn produce healthy cellular activity.

Artistically Express Rather Than Repress

Each of us are born to be artisans of personal expression. There is no greater joy than freeing our energy from emotional prison.

When it's not possible to be in nature, we can surround our environment with plants, fountains, gemstones, music and a variety of essential oils.

100% pure essential oils can actually bypass the blood brain barrier, rapidly absorb and interact with receptors in the central nervous system to help support healing. These essences so refined they're able to penetrate through the olfactory receptors (sense of smell) to the limbic (emotional center) of the brain. They also penetrate to the hippocampus, which is associated with the storage of working memory and short-term memory, and the pineal gland, which is often associated with spiritual development.

Simply by breathing in the pure scent of lavender or rose, as well as holding a pure quartz crystal in our hands, our sensory experience can transform our internal landscape.

Intaking pure water flushes stress and toxins out of the body, keeping us chemically balanced and internally fluid. Nature is our best psychologist if we slow ourselves down enough to truly take in the power of its earth medicine.

Dancing to rhythmic or tribal beats allows our primal spirit to come out to play as we release our stuck energy. Who said emotional release work can't be fun? As a matter of fact, we should laugh in the face of it, because anything that makes us feel unloved is a joke!

Many of us have learned to be 'troopers' and stoic instead of expressive. What fun is that? It's important to cry when moved to do so, to breathe deeply and fully and emphasize a giant release of our emotions via the out-breath. Shallow breathing actually causes us to hold in stuck emotions and is thought to be a major contributor to the proliferation of degenerative diseases in the body. When nothing else is possible given the situation, breathe and exhale!

Smiling: Your Hidden Superpower

Have you ever noticed how attractive and even magnetic people are who regularly smile? They can cause others to smile spontaneously as if they hold the grand secret to happiness. Smiling as a regular practice, holds multi-dimensional powers. Here's why:

Our states of happiness are either active or passive. So, instead of waiting for circumstances to make us happy, we can create habits in our lives that intentionally produce a blend of neurochemicals to flow such as dopamine, serotonin, oxytocin and endorphins. These become the neurotransmitters in our brain that chemically influence our states of happiness.

The simple act of smiling is one of the most powerful activators of this neurochemical cocktail in the brain. Because of this, smiling can also serve as a natural anti-depressant and pain reliever.

And clearly, we're better-looking when we smile! When we smile people treat us differently. We're viewed as more attractive, more reliable, peaceful and sincere.

Neuropsychologia, an International Journal in Behavioral and Cognitive Neuroscience, published a study on the effects of someone viewing an attractive, smiling face. A person smiling toward another was found to activate the viewer's orbitofrontal cortex, the region in the brain that processes sensory rewards.

This suggests that when we view a person smiling, we actually feel rewarded. So, when we ourselves smile, we're not only stimulating our own neurochemical cocktail, we have the gratification of positively affecting others. This enhances our self-worth by generating positive emotional associations with those around us.

How do we begin the act of smiling beyond our comfort zone? We need to become unstuck. It begins by expressing our emotions in fun, playful ways which creates a cellular release of our stuck energy. As the emotions in our cells become freed, smiling becomes a natural form of self-expression.

Singing, dancing, humming and even growling out our emotions provides us with a cellular release. It can renew our spirit and help us gain perspective that we're living and acting out precious moments in time. So why not make our moments an artistic expression of our multi-dimensional self? Is it any wonder that music, with its many nuances, inspires a palette of emotions that influence our lives on so many levels?

Falling in Love with Our Brain

Looking more deeply into our neurology, we discover how profoundly our brain shapes our perceptions and makes us uniquely who we are. The human brain itself contains nearly one-hundred-billion neurons along with hundreds of trillions of connections between those neurons. Our brain interacts with other brains, which comprises an estimated 700 billion neurons. One might say that the human brain is like a vast galaxy.

We carry this incredibly intricate organ wherever we go. In addition to filtering our perceptions, it tells our body systems how to function and move. It houses our powers of recall, reasoning and articulation. Each brain is vastly unique. It is a vessel for our soul's distinctive self-expression. The grand mystery to be discovered is how to unlock our brain's higher levels of potential.

Renowned psychiatrist and author of *Unleash the Power of the Female Brain*, Daniel Amen, MD speaks of 'falling in love with our brain.' He's states that females have radically more brain activity than men. The advantage to this is that we have amazing powers of perception and an astounding capacity for multi-tasking. The challenge is that our brains never rest. We're always making 'to do' lists. We worry more than men and are more sensitized to life's complexities.

Restoring Natural Order in Our Lives

One way we can love our brain and give it a rest is to clear the clutter out of our lives; to simplify, organize and make room for spaciousness as a personal lifestyle. This allows us to be more present, peaceful and purposeful.

Daily, our bodies are bombarded with toxins. From house cleaners to perfumes, pesticides and EMF toxicity, our organs and brain cells absorb and retain these toxins which then contribute to disease and skew our perceptions. Optimal brain health mandates a more natural, eco-conscious lifestyle for supporting longevity and mental clarity.

Daily, we become sum total of our accumulated life choices. Knowing how powerful this idea is, we can change the quality of our choices and create a refreshing new result for our lives.

It Starts with a Vision

You may have heard the saying, "Life without vision is nothing more than television." Sadly, many people discover late in life that their lives have vastly become the result of a cascading set of imposing circumstances that have nothing to do with their vision.

Some folks are born with a sense of destiny while others develop their life vision along the way. Circumstances outside of our control can also lead us to our destiny, while others detour us from our path. The key is to discern how our happiness, our sense of purpose and our relationships are benefitting as result of our life circumstances. We can then recalibrate as the need calls for it.

Emotional Resilience in Relationships

As long as we're in human form, we will inevitably interact with people and circumstances that will challenge our levels of emotional equanimity. As soon as we feel we've mastered an emotion, something may present itself that will shake us to our core.

In his book, *Emotional Resilience*, David Viscott speaks of the importance of transforming our toxic nostalgia. In other words, in order to avoid the accumulation of toxic nostalgia, we must communicate to others when we experience hurtful behavior by them. The key is to directly address the offensive behavior to the source close to the time that it happened in a manner that is self-honoring, objective and respectful to all concerned.

By doing so, we can become emotionally resilient rather than emotionally stuck. By avoidance, hurt can recoil into feelings of repression, anger, guilt, self-condemnation and ultimately, self-destruction in one form or another.

At times, I've found that when someone has behaved toward me in a condescending or hurtful manner, it has been a shock to my system simply because I don't operate that way. So, I've found myself temporarily experiencing a form of emotional paralysis in the face of adversity.

I'll take a moment to reflect as to whether something a person has said or done is a true offense, or whether it has triggered an old wound I need to heal within me. I've learned to process my feelings during meditation or in nature to gain a clearer perspective.

I'm then empowered to express myself to the person, if needed, from a more heart-centered place. Letter writing is also a great way to communicate with those who tend to be defensive or confrontational. Upholding our core values without finger-pointing toward the other's shortcomings is a great of self-love practice.

Talk to the Hand, Talk to the Heart!

Accepting ownership of how a statement or behavior impacted us while explaining the standard of how we expect to be treated, allows the other person to reflect upon their behavior and accept ownership for their actions without confrontation or humiliation.

Using this as a continued self-love practice, it's easier to stand up for ourselves with internal strength the moment an offensive situation occurs. The evolution of this practice will result in a clearer magnetic field within you and me which makes space for us to view situations with more objectivity and humor.

The state of victimhood is so institutionalized in our culture that it has become part of our collective belief spiral where we commonly classify our roles in difficult situations in the form of the 'victim or perpetrator,' underlying fear or guilt. It is time for liberation!

We're in this together! It's important to have self-compassion for the difficult situations we've endured while we also transform our attitude that has shaped our world view into an 'us and them' mentality. Individuals who behave poorly have their own story of pain behind their actions, we can only control our reaction to them.

We're each here to experience ourselves as unique facets of a quantum world that is continually reflecting back to us and to one another, varied, fascinating aspects of our collective human story.

Positive Self-Talk

> *No longer will I accept crumbs from the table.*
> *I'm the banquet, baby!*
> — *Christina*

By the nature of being human, we may still find ourselves at times struggling with negative self-talk by the hidden wounded self. A highly effective technique for transforming old patterns from our cellular 'record keeper' is to daily reinforce positive self-talk, personal affirmations and actions that support empowering new behavior and positively charged emotions.

For instance, in response to the earlier discussed accumulated beliefs stemming from being unwanted at birth, we could say or pray:

I now see that I've been holding myself in captivity with feelings of guilt and shame for being born; and that I've felt unworthy of love. I also recognize that I've allowed others to determine my worthiness.

I am releasing from my heart, my mind, my DNA and my cellular awareness, the cause, effect, record and memory of these unwholesome beliefs and feelings. Grand Creator of all Life, re-pattern within me the absolute knowing of my worthiness and the confidence to live out my highest value in this lifetime.

An affirmation of resolution could sound like this:

I am a brilliant child of Creation, born of love and providence. Daily, I am attracting the persons, places and things that support me, my brilliance and my passions in the highest and best way. I am actively bringing my best self forward while uplifting and inspiring others along the way.

SELF-LOVE RITUAL

Eye-to-Eye with Your Soul

This is one of the most profound exercises one can experience and yet ironically, for many, it's a frightening one. It can sometimes seem too exposing to directly commune with our soul by gazing into our own eyes and facing the brilliance of our inner truth. It's time to bring these fears to the light, knowing that a life of impassioned living awaits a brave heart!

In a moment of privacy, stand or sit in front of a wall mirror. Take a few deep breaths and gaze into your own eyes. Do not look away. In your peripheral vision, observe your face encasing your eyes and appreciate yourself as a sculpture of the divine beholding you with unconditional love.

Look into your eyes as you would look into the eyes of a loved one. Smile; let your heart open with compassion, encouragement and honesty. Tell your soul, *I love you, (say your name). I appreciate your journey. I appreciate all that you have experienced in order to find me again. I'm here to support you with all my love.*

Tell your soul what you are experiencing. Allow your soul to speak back to you. As you continue the practice of soul-gazing and speaking to your soul as a dear trusted friend, you'll be amazed at the wisdom that comes forth.

If you're tempted to place attention on your perceived flaws and you begin harshly judging yourself, allow your spirit to become playful rather than destructive. Your soul is magnificent and multidimensional. Even amidst the trials and tribulations of your life, it lovingly upholds the grandeur of your full potential self.

The key is to affirm your connection with your own internal knower:

I am a beautiful woman whose experiences have sculpted themselves on my soul, my face and my body. I bless the evidence of my life lessons as my badges of courage! I use them as vehicles of perspective for reuniting with my core purpose as I shine with greater brilliance.

Each morning, look into your eyes and give yourself a pep talk:

This is going to be my best day ever! I am moving forward as my beautiful, brilliant, generous and courageous self—all that I am and aspire to be, it is activated now!

You can be creative with your own transformational language as it pertains to any area of your life. Smile generously at yourself! Nourish your soul with your happy neurochemicals. Smile internally at your organs, tissues and bones. Then turn your smile outward to uplift, heal and inspire others.

Observe how magic and synchronicities becomes palpable as a natural order for your life. Experience a miraculous upliftment of your self-worth!

CHAPTER THREE
REWARDING THE HEROINE

I don't believe people are looking for the meaning of life as much as they are looking for the experience of being 'alive.'

— Joseph Campbell

CHAPTER THREE
REWARDING THE HEROINE

We, as women are heroic beings. We're cause-driven. We're survivors and master navigators through adversity. We're supreme multi-taskers. We have given of ourselves so that others may thrive, often at the expense of our own well-being.

A new paradigm for the empowered woman includes high levels of self-expression and self-fulfillment, thus moving us into a juicier place of thriving rather than surviving.

Because it's our natural tendency as women to give, even when we're depleted, we need to assert ourselves toward self-love. Our self-depleting tendencies are replaced by self-replenishment. By filling our own cup as wise contemporary goddesses, we'll have plenty of resources to give to others as we are inspired to or as the need calls for it. The act of giving then comes from a place that is rich with internal resources, thus completing the circle of life.

Understanding the Heroine's Journey

In his book, *The Hero with a Thousand Faces*, mythologist Joseph Campbell describes 'the hero's journey' as a process for souls to discover themselves through a series of life cycles. As with many ancient myths, storytelling was predominantly postured to reflect the journey of men, even when interpreted by Joseph Campbell.

In his later years, he acknowledged this shortcoming, stating that in ancient times, writers of mythology were usually men who had excessive time on their hands to spin stories about themselves while dutiful women were focused on teaching their children. He stated,

Women were too busy; they had too damn much to do to sit around thinking about stories.

Thus, I've taken the liberty to reinterpret the steps of 'The Hero's Journey' to bring meaning to 'The Heroine's Journey' as it applies to self-love and a woman's goddess nature. It's the grand formula great stories and movies are made of. As we discover how this formula applies to our own story, we may more swiftly redeem it.

The Heroine begins her journey, departing from her familiar world of external gratifications. She's summoned from within to enter a supernatural place of curious powers and events—her soul's call to an inner adventure (answering to her innate brilliance). Often, the heroine initially refuses the inner prompting by crafting a myriad of excuses. Nonetheless, the journey is inevitable.

As the Heroine accepts the invitation, she crosses the first threshold. She plunges into her shadow self, abandoning her feminine essence and struggling to uphold herself within a predominantly masculine culture (her struggle with self-love).

Her initiation begins as she enters a road of trials. At times, she perceives herself as facing these trials alone. She then reacquaints herself with her inner guidance and learns to trust it to light her way (her reconnection with her higher-self).

Later, she discovers the miraculous invisible forces supporting her throughout her journey. She then meets face to face, her Inner Goddess, the archetype of her Feminine Full Potential Self and learns to honor her calling. The invisible miraculously becomes palpable and she is replenished by the all-encompassing power of unconditional love (she is empowered by self-love).

As she continues on her journey, she encounters a temptress, who serves as the doubter, seeking to derail her from her path. She must make the ultimate choice to continue the Heroine's journey or return to mediocrity. This is where the Heroine enters a symbolic phase of atonement with the father (facing self-doubt).

The father is a terrifying patriarchal archetype that reveals itself as an authority figure over her life or may show up as her own inner critic who overpowers her inner sensibilities, causing her a sense of separation from her core knowing (dark night of the soul).

Will the Heroine, as the newly empowered woman, embrace her wholeness, or remain a victim of circumstances by giving up her inner power to the authority, or perpetrator that conflicts with her core knowing? Will she give her power to the false prophet, or her ego, that keeps her separate from Spirit? In her atonement with the father, she dies to the ego (lesser self), leaving the shining wisdom of her Essential Self to guide her (her surrender to a higher power).

This process represents the alchemical transformation of the soul.

At last, the Heroine has achieved the boon of heightened attainment from her journey. As she faces new trials upon her return, she must now choose to return with her boon or not. She must achieve a balance between the inner and outer domains and her masculine-feminine nature, retaining and integrating her new-found wisdom in the ordinary world (pursuing her life purpose amidst the tide of mediocrity).

As she applies the boon to her daily living, she lives in the present more fully and fearlessly. Through her endurance she achieves the transformative power of her renewed life purpose (an empowered woman).

Endurance is not to be mistaken with long-suffering. As women, endurance holds true the power of our personal sovereignty as we overcome adversity and ultimately achieve our sacred purpose. Long-suffering, on the other hand, tends to negate our personal sovereignty in order to concede to the agenda of others.

Some of us have become habitually long-suffering even toward ourselves, as we endlessly endeavor to measure up to a worthiness standard that never quite hits the mark. We may therefore suffer in vain, never allowing ourselves to enjoy the privileges in life that others do. Even though this is a self-demeaning behavior, it can seem so justifiable at times, at which point we become the authors of our own undoing.

Catching Negative Self-Talk in the Act

At times, we may convince ourselves we are unworthy of love by saying, *If-only I didn't have this flaw, I'd be worthy enough to attract a meaningful love relationship in my life.* If the flaw was fixed, we might find another reason why we're not good enough. Or, we may find ourselves continuing an inherited belief from our upbringing or even from our ancestors by echoing, *In-order for life to be meaningful, I must suffer.*

The point is, we may have forgotten our inherent worthiness, simply by entering a human body from otherworldly realms. Out of nothing we became a spark, a grand idea in the mind of God, filled with free agency. We hold within us absolute divine beauty and genius! This is our inheritance. We've simply forgotten how to claim it for ourselves and access its unlimited potential.

It begins by fostering high levels of self-respect and modeling this behavior for others to follow. Even if we have endured shock and trauma beyond our control, we have within us, the power to heal our wounds, change our minds and our fields of attraction.

We must fervently disable the groove within our minds that believes we are permanently damaged. Unhealed beliefs can skew our perceptions during subsequent unrelated situations that may arise. Simply by the tone of someone's voice, a look by them, even their scent can trigger a deep and latent emotional response that has been unresolved from within us. The tools in this book are designed for identifying and healing our core wounds and defusing the triggers.

The Power of Knowing When to Say "No"

As we champion our capacity to 'choose' as wise goddesses do, we are modeling self-love. We become inaccessible to the assaults of disrespect or abuse, whether it is physical, sexual, verbal, psychological or monetary. We are no longer powerless to a fearsome authoritarian force outside ourselves. Instead, we are wise and empowered guardians of our energy.

Another aspect of taking care of ourselves is listening and responding to our instincts that alert us when we're in danger. We may have a prompting within us that says *I need to remove myself from this situation now!* We must trust it and move decisively when our intuition speaks rather than justify or excuse an unwholesome situation in order to be polite or appease the expectations of others.

Rather than harboring abuse as a shameful secret, we can stand for our virtue, seek support from loved ones and remove ourselves strategically and decisively from the situation. Abusers must be held accountable once we've found refuge in a safe environment. At no time should we allow ourselves to be long-suffering in the face of abuse, period.

I strongly recommend to all women, that they pursue their own independent sources of income and establish a personal emergency savings or investment account—even if they are content in a financially secure marriage. A woman's financial solvency secured by a personal nest egg in her name assures her a life raft in response to unforeseen circumstances. It also gives her the confidence to make self-empowered choices in the face of adversity.

Mentors and Female Bonding

Surround yourself only with people who are
going to lift you higher.
-- Oprah Winfrey

As women, it's essential to align our-selves with peers who have cultivated strong levels of self-worth and happiness in their daily lives—those who have set their course in a direction that values and supports the success of others.

We know these individuals as mentors; ones who show us higher ways than we have known before. As we study their practices with an open mind and heart and interpret these practices for our own lives, we can significantly accelerate our progress.

We've each come into this world gifted with free agency to rise above our circumstances. We possess the ability to be internal shape-shifters and bring about change in our lives which in turn, affects the lives of others. By taking stock of the limiting beliefs we have bought into in the past, we can swiftly recognize the counterintuitive energies we've set into motion, and then quickly recalibrate ourselves in a more positive direction.

We are essentially saying to the universe:

I recognize how truly powerful I AM. I'm now aware of how impactful my beliefs and emotions are which have to date driven my behaviors. I can take this same essential energy to reshape my life, beginning by establishing a new set of beliefs and subsequent actions.

Another important part of the journey toward wholeness is having individuals in our lives with whom we can confide.

I love getting together with my girlfriends. We speak the same language. We don't need to explain ourselves…we just know. No matter what country we're from, no matter what our upbringing or personal interests are, when women get together with the intention of bonding and supporting one another, very quickly we will find the common denominators that make us one.

While for most of us, the men in our lives drive our passions and motivate us to become the best we can be, it is the women in our lives that allow us to 'let it all hang out,' to be sad or be silly as only girls can be, to serve as sounding boards for our heart aches, and to midwife our soul's evolution to a higher place.

The ancient tradition of women's healing circles is once again emerging throughout the world as a means for women to bear their souls and support one another during various passages of their lives. While soul-healing is an inside job, it is comforting to know that we don't have to go through every layer of the journey alone.

Life would be incomplete for a woman without the presence of healthy male relationships and friendships. There are many wonderful men in the world who desire to be with women who are modeling self-referred love. Not only is it an inspiration to them, it's sexy. And, it brings out the best in them.

As a powerful, feminine woman you can bring out the best in your masculine companions (straight or gay) and become someone who can be trusted as they endeavor to bring themselves to a higher place. Each of us is on an important journey. Exchanging interest and excitement in each other's process can be a delicious and creative adventure! Including healthy masculine relationships into your life equation is an essential part of the feminine healing journey.

Aloneness to All-Oneness

When a woman experiences loneliness she may find herself sinking into a hole of depression that she must literally catapult herself from! Or, she may find herself wandering from person to person, social venue to social venue, to find validation of her soul's worth. In either case, it's imperative for her to define and exemplify her core values and seek out the company of those who resonate with those values.

By continually cultivating our core values and seeking out activities that support those values, we begin to foster the attraction principle that exemplifies the 'quality' in relationships rather than the 'quantity,' even if for a season, we experience periods of aloneness. Aloneness for a season can provide a meaningful venue for establishing clarity and our all-oneness with God. Sometimes aloneness can bring us to a profoundly creative place where the inner revelations and inspirations of the soul are born.

The key is to become balanced. Too much aloneness and extensive isolation can be destructive. At times, we must simply take a break from the reflective path and go out, shake it up and have fun! It's important to let loose for no reason or justification!!!

We don't need permission or approval, nor do we have to work tirelessly in order to deserve time out to celebrate with others. Play is the natural instinct of the soul. Many productive relationships and ideas spring forth as a result of play.

After a long period of living alone, I elected to put my belongings in storage, travel and visit friends for a few months. One of my stops along the way was to stay with a group of friends living together whom chronologically, would be categorized as 'senior citizens.' From an energetic standpoint, this label couldn't be farther from the truth. They are some of the most playful and expressive people in my circle of acquaintances. They continually shake up my world with their fun medicine.

One early morning at 7:00am, my then 75-year old female friend got dressed and went downstairs for breakfast (while I was still waking from my slumber). I heard her singing a melody with wild abandon when suddenly her 65-year old male housemate approached her with a giant lion's *Rooaarr!* She responded with a dramatic shrill of surprise, and then roared back, beating her chest and exclaiming, *This is MY world! Rooaarr! I'm going to kick-ass today...take that!*

They were laughing and carrying on like two excited children full of mischief. As a result of their continual lifestyle of play, they are unmistakably radiant, healthy...and joyful.

SELF-LOVE RITUAL

Activating Your PEA Brain!

Just as there are many neurochemicals that become activated when we smile, those same chemicals and more become activated within our body when we fall in love. The euphoria we feel in the presence of love bypasses the radar of our rational mind, and so profoundly affects our state of being that we often find ourselves living and operating in another dimension.

The key then is learning how to activate and modulate these love chemicals within ourselves, whether we are falling in love with someone or not. Let's first take a look at these exotic potions:

Norepinephrine (or **Noradrenalin)** is a chemical that highly stimulates the neurons in our brain and accelerates our cellular activity, causing our heart to accelerate or 'skip a beat' as we call it, when we fall in love. Adrenaline-induced norepinephrine in the brain can heighten feelings of joy. It also can decrease appetite...sound familiar?

Dopamine is a neurochemical that sends messages from the brain's limbic system into the body. As a precursor to norepinephrine, dopamine activates our reward circuitry and the pleasure system of our brain, providing feelings of enjoyment. It motivates us and increases our social abilities. It also can induce the release of its counterparts; the mood-elevating, rest-inducing serotonin and oxytocin, also known as the bonding chemical or the unconditional love hormone associated with nurturing and generous affection.

Phenylethylamine or (PEA) serves as a releasing agent and modulator of norepinephrine and dopamine. As this chemical cocktail combines together, we feel the euphoric and the energizing chemistry of love. PEA, therefore, has a unique ability to enhance our innate sexuality, reverse aging and restore more youthful mental and physical functions. It is a research-proven mood-brightener that can quickly lift the lows of depression, sadness, hopelessness and discouragement.

By activating these love potions, we can actually learn how to fall in love with ourselves, along with expanding our capacity to love and cherish others in a more meaningful way. Imagine what it would be like to continuously have a love affair with life!

Try these daily rituals for transforming the chemical cocktail within you and enhancing your PEA levels:

- Loving Eye Contact: Yes, studies have shown that your body's PEA is enhanced, simply by a loving gaze into the eyes of another. It is a dual PEA charge for you as well as your gazing counterpart. You can also lovingly gaze into your own eyes (via the mirror) to percolate PEA within you.

- Detox and Balance: Remove toxic thoughts from your mind and toxic chemicals from your body. Include a daily diet of positive thought and affirmative action, along with consuming plenty of pure (preferably spring or micronized) water, organic fresh fruits and leafy greens. These components will alkalize your body and increase enzymatic activity while also enhancing your ability to produce and process the good chemicals you desire.

- Consume a PEA Rich Diet: High-protein plant foods contain some of the richest sources of phenylalanine, including blue-green algae, raw organic soybeans, lentils, chickpeas, flaxseed, peanuts, almonds, walnuts and tahini (made from stone-ground sesame seeds). Pink salmon, free range grain-fed eggs, sheep and goat milk/cheese, cow cheddar cheese and human milk also contain PEA.

- Consume Dark Chocolate: Dark chocolate is nature's luscious superfood. It contains more than 500 natural chemical compounds, including the mood-elevating and pleasure-inducing PEA, which explains why love and chocolate have a deep correlation. It's known to have one of the highest anti-oxidant ORAC factors of all foods. Its high magnesium content promotes relaxation, explaining why women often crave chocolate when stressed or hormonal. Avoid commercial chocolates with high sugar content. Experience the sheer magic of consuming raw cacao beans or chocolate bars with at least a 72% pure cacao content. Organic, fair-trade chocolate is best.

- Exercise and Breath: PEA can be activated by both. Research has shown that depressed people show low levels of PEA which explains why exercise is a natural anti-depressant. Exercise penetrates and oxygenates the brain barrier, causing a natural high.

- Enhance Your Dance: Not only is dance a creative form of exercise, it has the ability to activate your brain's pleasure centers, enhancing dopamine and oxytocin. Dance can also kindle flirtation and eye contact which percolates your PEA pleasure chemicals. Flirtation is fun! It can also enhance self-esteem when modulated in a wise and classy way.

CHAPTER FOUR
RECLAIMING OUR BIRTHRIGHT

*Nothing is impossible. The word itself says
"I'm possible!"*

— Audrey Hepburn

CHAPTER FOUR
RECLAIMING OUR BIRTHRIGHT

Kicking Out the False Prophets

Our birthright is to be happy and shine; even laugh at life's absurdities! Every day is our birthday, as we're continually giving birth to a new dimension of ourselves. Taking life too seriously is yet another curse of the guilty. It's another lie of the false prophet within us that says, *In-order for life to be meaningful, I must suffer.* It's time for each of us to kick out the false prophets in our own domain, and let the inner comedian take center stage.

Behavior modification practices have been imposed on us from the very early stages of our lives. To our earliest recollections, we were taught to sit still and be quiet in school when our bodies may have inspired us to move, and our bright spirits may have prompted us to express ourselves.

Most of us, as children, instinctively knew when we were being indoctrinated and constrained by the false prophets of a mechanized system which is counterintuitive to our soul's innate expressions. Yet at such an impressionable stage of life, we did not have the frame of reference by which to distinguish our inner sensibilities and claim our power.

This treacherous pattern of control by the school systems has in many cases become even more ingrained and continues to rob young souls of their core knowing. Some of the most brilliant and intuitive children I know have miserably flunked the standardized testing systems. Consequently, these precious souls have been led to believe that their level of intelligence is substandard, and they have failed to fit within the norms of society (as if that were a bad thing!)

The entertainment industry continues to be a powerful tool for providing a window into the wonders of the world and the magical realms of life. In many ways it significantly contributes to the positive transformation and the evolution of society and wakes us up to slices of life we might otherwise be ignorant to.

It has also done a masterful job of broadcasting the continued, indulgent meanderings of dysfunction, violence and horror—and glamorizing it as art.

As a society, we've become woefully addicted to this form of intrigue, and often view other light-hearted artistic expressions as trite and less worthy of artistic merit.

Aggression programming, especially consumed by our youth through the gaming industry and the proliferation of violent movies, can potentiate an indifference to violence. Our society at large is becoming increasingly desensitized to healthy social behavior due to a mass preoccupation with information-overload through our multimedia lifestyles in the form of television, movies, video games, computers and portable media devices.

As much as our technological advancements have assisted our evolution in positive ways, we must also recognize their contribution to the ills of society.

As emerging empowered women, it's essential to practice and model a healthy balance between our relationship with all facets of modern technology and our personal, primal relationships with humans, animals and nature.

Re-igniting Our Original Joy

A belly laugh increases the ability of your
immune system to fight infections.
— Elizabeth Taylor, Professor

Whatever violations have pierced our life experiences, no one or no-thing can touch the original joy that resides within the soul! Joy is the essence that fuels our sacred purpose in life. We simply need to remove the negative programming from our internal and external hard drives that has woven, layer by layer a set of unwholesome life laws which have formerly run our show.

When we take time for reflection and develop the practice of soul listening, we become profoundly aware of the brilliance and beauty that resides within us. Self-honesty followed by forgiveness toward ourselves and others, can lift our spirits and free our energies to pursue our passions. Freely pursuing our passions draws us into the realm of miracles as the natural order of living.

As we progress, we may still occasionally find ourselves facing limiting beliefs that have driven our life choices. For instance, if we've set a law into motion that says, *All men have bad intentions,* we will undoubtedly attract men into our life who resonate and corroborate with this internal law. As we begin shape-shifting our beliefs and reinforcing a positive new network of internal laws, we will similarly attract people and circumstances into our lives that reinforce our higher states of evolution.

How about employing the expression of gratitude in present time? As we express gratitude for the qualities and events we desire to attract into our lives, we're essentially holding up our cup of opportunity to be filled. For example, we can fill ourselves with this affirmation: *I am so grateful to have wonderful, respectful men in my life who honor and support me; who recognize my core essence and are open to receiving the same support from me.*

Rather than petitioning a reluctant deity, we're acknowledging our co-creative relationship with our Creator, and the unlimited power of the universe to bless our lives with our heart's desires. Repetition of this practice generates momentum for attracting positive results and transforms our cellular magnetism.

Healthy Inquiry and Modeling New Behavior

When we find ourselves impacted by the behavior of others, it's important to keep in mind that other people are also living their lives according to their own acquired internal laws. Individuals can operate from wholesome laws in some aspects of their lives where they embody high self-esteem, and at other times, act out from another set of unwholesome laws based on a set of wounded beliefs.

Part of the life journey includes the discovery of our dual behaviors, which contrast our healthy core values with our wounded core beliefs in need of transformation.

For instance, you or I may know someone who is a rock star in their professional life, yet exhibits dysfunctional behavior or even inhibitions towards others, in more intimate situations.

A nurse, for example, may have carved out a fulfilling career as a model caretaker for others, while at home she is burdened by her wounded core belief that she is unworthy of self-love, spiraling her into self-sabotaging, addictive behaviors that impact her entire family.

We are constantly modeling behavior. The questions are: Are we modeling our own self-referred behavior, or the imposed behavior of others? Whose thoughts are we thinking? Are we entertaining our own self-nurturing thoughts? Or, are we channeling the electromagnetic-field of thoughts swarming around us by others?

Rather than react to another's unwholesome laws and subsequent behaviors, we can strengthen our discernment by referring to our core values. This practice gives us a keener ability to uphold others in a positive framework while at the same time, become more personally empowered.

As we begin to view the behavior of others with a state of inquiry rather than by a reactive response, we find ourselves becoming creative solution-finders. Positively reframing our own emotions in respect to the behavior of others frees our energies from unwholesome entanglement and gives us the resources to respond more nobly from a clearer perspective.

As long as we are sojourners in the human terrain, there are times when we may still find ourselves suddenly straying from mindfulness and acting out unconsciously. We may behave in a way that surprises and causes disappointment within us.

Rather than amplifying our displeasure with self-condemnation, we can immediately course-correct. We can use each lesson and its impact to gain greater wisdom, realign with our core values and attain a renewed perspective by which to assist others on their journey. It's important for each of us to look at our lives and our choices as an evolutionary voyage fueled by compassion toward ourselves and others.

SELF-LOVE RITUAL

Igniting Your Solar Field

Your navel centered within the body's solar plexus region is your umbilical 'core' connection to the universal life force. It was your gestational portal that received sustenance from your earth mother inside her womb and continues to serve you today as your portal of connection to the universal womb of creation.

Your solar plexus chakra, or spiritual center located in the solar plexus region is innately bonded with your core consciousness. It is an information gateway and emotional record keeper that continually intakes the accountings of our life experiences. It serves as the seat of the soul that encodes the hidden messages of your ancestral history, passed down from generation to generation.

Have you ever noticed that your navel is highly sensitive to touch as if it were the forbidden zone in your body? This is due to the highly charged emotional spiral it holds, along with its history that may fear its disturbance.

Fear is the host of our unresolved, emotionally layered dimensions, housed in your body's solar plexus. The navel serves as the seed storehouse of these records of emotion. Its exposure is inevitable because your soul is accelerating on your evolutionary path. Most importantly, you can recognize your own fears and reawaken the power of your solar consciousness, bringing your fears to the light. You can then recalibrate your emotional drivers to strengthen and free up your emotional capacities.

There is no mistaking that the internal record keeper in each of us is called the solar plexus. Within its name, lies the solution. 'Solar' means 'sun,' and 'plexus' means a 'network of vessels in the body.' These two bring together a cosmology of body and soul.

I'm suggesting that our genetic code is not etched in stone as the old laws of science would purport. Rather, new scientific breakthroughs reveal that our DNA, in part, can be malleable according to our own evolutionary process. I believe we can accelerate this process by wisely using our external light source, the Sun, to ignite our solar field beginning in the core of our solar plexus. The Sun can charge our network of vessels with light and transport our awareness into higher realms.

I invite you to use these daily steps to accelerate your Solar Field. They will nourish your physical body, bathe your cells with light, and transform the burdensome emotional spiral of secrecy into a joyous, heightened level of transparency and authenticity. Solar Wisdom can increase your level of optimism and transpose this spiral of the shadow self.

- Studies have shown that a large number of women today are significantly deficient in the Vitamin D3 which is linked to depression, low immunity and a number of other ailments. Vitamin D deficiency is largely caused by sunlight deficiency and over-exposure to electromagnetic fields generated by computers and other electronics. It's helpful to add Vitamin D3 to your nutritional program if your life has been imbalanced by the abovementioned lifestyle.

- Consider making friends with the sun rather than regarding it as a continual threat. Wisely measured sun exposure can be a lifesaver on multiple levels. The sun's natural photosynthesis of Vitamin D3 boosts immunity and endocrine function, increases bone density and is a natural mood elevator. Each of us is responsible to use common sense as pertains to our constitutional skin types and understand the risks of overexposure to the suns UV rays.

If you are fair skinned, photosensitive or are on prescription medications, it is advised to speak with your health care professional about appropriate levels of sun exposure and adding Vitamin D3 supplements to your diet.

- The sun's healing rays are assimilated through your eyes, skin and the solar plexus region of the body. Allow yourself to occasionally remove your sun glasses and let the sun's indirect reflections to gently bathe your eyes. Unless you are an adept and knowledgeable sun gazer, avoid direct gazing at the sun. Consider a daily diet of at least 10 minutes twice per day in the sun, exposing your solar plexus region to its healing rays while placing your body on Mother Earth. Welcome the uplifting and healing power of the sun's warm light transmissions into your being.

- Supplement your sun diet with nutritious sun-infused lemon water first thing in the morning along with other nutritious photo-synthesized fresh organic fruits, leafy greens and sprouts throughout the day. Sun tea or fresh sun-infused herbal beverages are a great way to enjoy tea without brewing. Place a glass container of fresh, edible herbs and pure water into the sun for one hour and drink!

- Give yourself a loving aromatherapy belly rub. Buy some pure organic grapefruit essential oil, place a couple of drops into your hands and inhale its vapors, then gently rub it into your solar plexus. Pause and allow it to penetrate. Grapefruit, along with other citrus fruits are visibly sun foods, evidenced by the patterns inside a citrus appearing like the rays of the sun. The essential oils of citrus, and particularly grapefruit, are known to penetrate the olfactory system and significantly uplift the psyche. Its placement on the solar plexus can penetrate the deeper levels of the emotional psyche.

- Next, use your favorite unscented lotion or oil as a base for massaging your solar plexus; first in a gentle counter-clockwise motion as you inhale, followed by a circular clockwise motion on the exhale. As you inhale, identify your fears and other unwanted emotions. Let it go deep. Pause and visualize your inner sun penetrating your belly, moving through your network of vessels, filling your body with light and increasing your solar field. Exhale and release your fears and unwanted tension. Repeat as often as desired.

- In Sanskrit the solar plexus chakra is known as Manipura, the third chakra primarily associated with self-esteem, confidence and willpower. A balanced Manipura chakra enables you to have sovereignty over your thoughts and emotional responses, set healthy boundaries and be at peace with yourself. Its physical association is with digestive function, so it stands to reason that what we energetically take in and digest will undoubtedly affect our physical digestion. Healthy alliances combined with healthy nutrition are extremely important for fostering healthy bodily functions.

- A regular yoga practice with asanas focused on core strength is ideal for Manipura healing and balancing. Warrior Pose is the easiest yoga asana for opening Manipura. Holding it for a few minutes every morning while facing the sun will begin to open your solar plexus.

- Increase your core strength. Go about your daily activities and consciously and repetitively tighten (exhale) and release (inhale) your belly muscles. Integrate yoga and other core energizing practices into your life. Move from the core, dance from the core, breathe from the core, live according to your core principles. You will activate your chi (or energy source,) and positively affect your magnetic field of attraction.

By practicing these simple sun rituals, you will find yourself becoming increasingly optimistic, energetic and clear minded.

CHAPTER FIVE

LEARNING FROM SEASONED, EMPOWERED WOMEN

The most difficult thing
is the decision to act,
the rest is merely tenacity.
The fears are paper tigers.
You can do anything you decide to do.
...The process is its own reward.

— Amelia Earhart

CHAPTER FIVE
LEARNING FROM SEASONED, EMPOWERED WOMEN

We often admire empowered women as noted leaders or celebrities, yet there are many wise and courageous women who contently live their lives as unsung heroes. Empowered women know that the journey of life itself has its own reward. They are fueled by their passions and their commitment to an inner calling that speaks above the chatter of trivial pursuits. Yet, often the outcome of such pursuits results in notoriety and great admiration by others.

Empowered women are committed to generating love relationships. They know that a cause that brings healing, inspiration and equality to others is a cause worth fighting for. Empowered women often venture into worlds where they aren't accepted and pave a new way where there once was none. These women prevail amidst the tides of adversity.

They've had to create their own life raft, when at times they felt that they were sinking. Their life raft is their own self-referred love and affirmative action. They are driven by a purpose that is greater than themselves and therefore draw inspiration from higher dimensions. They celebrate their successes, small and large and celebrate the success of others with equal value.

Allow me to share the inspirations I have gained from three empowered, self-made women. They have forged very different paths, yet they share the commonality of having yielded extraordinary lives filled with the fruits of their love, endurance and devotion to their core purpose.

EMPOWERED WOMAN #1:

KATHY BUCKLEY

At the end of your day, shake off the labels you wore of being a mom, career woman, wife...or those pesky labels that say I'm not good enough. Take a bath. Soak into the essence of who you truly are and revel in it!
— *Kathy Buckley*

Mysteriously, at a very young age, Kathy became deaf. Specialists misinterpreted her poor performance in second grade as mental retardation, sending her to a school for retarded and physically impaired children. It took a slew of school experts and nearly a year of time to discover that her speech and language impediment was simply due to hearing loss.

Once properly addressed, she entered public school. Her intelligence and her height soared above her classmates. She was often isolated by her peers, however, and on one occasion, she was raped.

Holding this dark secret to herself, she persevered. She did some teenage modeling and studied fashion design, graduating from high school in 1972.

After high school, she said, *I went through one hell after another.*

Kathy suffered internal injuries from a car accident and required 32 stitches to her face.

Then in 1974 at the age of 20, Kathy was run over by a 3,500-pound lifeguard jeep while lying on her back on the beach at Mentor Headlands State Park in Ohio. The jeep crushed her chest and shoulder. She quips about the driver, *Talk-about not knowing what your job description is!*

She lived in and out of a wheelchair for more than two years and was ultimately impaired for five years due to the accident. The doctors told her she'd never walk again. She explained, *Well, I didn't hear the doctor, so I got up and walked out!*

She packed up her car and drove out west not knowing where she was going to land. She parked her car along the ocean and lived in her car for two months. She was on a quest to discover who she was amidst the insanity she had experienced.

A few years later, Kathy was diagnosed with cervical cancer and experienced two more grueling years of hospital visits. Her endurance got her through it and she moved on.

For her first 33 years (except for a few uncomfortable years with antiquated hearing aids) she got by on reading lips, a skill self-taught at a young age. Kathy learned to mimic the people she came in contact with. She boasts: *Some people think my hearing impairment is a handicap. Not me—whenever I'm with the Italian side of my family I have found it to be a total blessing. Do you know what it's like to be with a pack of Italians whose mouths are going 80 m.p.h.?*

Kathy later met her friend Geri Jewell who had cerebral palsy. There was a contest called: 'Stand-up Comics Take a Stand to Raise Money for United Cerebral Palsy.' She thought: *That would be a nice thing to do, just to help out. I did the contest thinking it was amateur night. Yet there were seasoned comics performing and this was my first time onstage. And I won! And I've been doing comedy ever since.*

It wasn't until the summer, when Buckley performed at the Hollywood Comedy Room in West Hollywood that she finally understood the power of her humor. For the first time in her budding career as a comedian her hearing aids were properly adjusted, and she could hear the audience laugh without the painful feedback from on-stage speakers. When she stepped off stage, she cried.

Kathy's fondest wish has been to achieve an entertainment name big enough, so people will listen as she advocates for people with disabilities. *As you start building a name,* she says, *you can use it to help make contributions back into society.*

She travels all over the country doing comedy shows and working for the government on behalf of the Americans with Disabilities Act (ADA). Buckley encourages people not to limit others.

Billed as 'America's First Hearing Impaired Comedienne,' Kathy's one-woman show, *DONT BUCK WITH ME!* chronicling her extraordinary life was a smashing success in Hollywood.

Soon Kathy began touring the U.S. playing major comedy venues. In record time she became one of the most popular comediennes in the country with material based on, among other things, her hearing loss.

Kathy's unique persona and platform also attracted high profile television appearances on *The Tonight Show* with Jay Leno; and national profiles on the *Today Show, Good Morning America,* and many other major network news shows. She was included in the E!

Entertainment Television Special: *The World's Most Intriguing Women.*

Her humor has a higher purpose. *My comedy disarms people,* says Kathy. *I love to make people laugh, but I love it even more if I can teach them something at the same time.*

Kathy backs her philosophy by tirelessly performing on behalf of nonprofit and educational organizations. She has hosted and appeared in benefits with numerous celebrities and has also guest appeared on some the most prestigious stages in the country. She was further recognized by the U.S. Air Force and U.S. Army for outstanding efforts toward disability employment awareness.

She entertains and enlightens people of all ages...but her heart belongs to children. One project that is dear to her own heart is her work with *No Limits,* an after-school program in Culver City, California for low income families as well as a *National Theater Group for Deaf and Hard of Hearing Children.* Kathy has been teaching deaf and hearing-impaired kids about self-esteem and lessons about life.

When I asked Kathy, what has kept her going through all of the adversities she has faced Kathy replied, *My-unwavering faith has gotten me through everything. I am grateful for all of my blessings. I've taken responsibility for my own needs, and I love to give. The children whose lives I've had the opportunity to impact in a positive way gives back to me...in the experience of great joy.*

When talking to her, a person can completely forget that she is deaf. To her, being deaf is just something that she's had to deal with. She doesn't let it stop her from living fully and making a difference in the world. To learn more: www.kathybuckley.com.

EMPOWERED WOMAN #2:

WOWZA

All of life is vibrating and it's all humming! Every atom and particle in the solar system is humming its own resonant tone. Call it God, spirit, divinity, or wholeness; 'The Truth is in the Tone.'
                                                        — Wowza

Wowza is my cherished, inspired friend -- internationally known by some and unknown by others. This is all about to change for a woman who is bringing the world an exceptional gift – the legacy of her life's work.

Wowza was brought up by stern parents who enforced what they considered a proper upbringing. Her mother became oppressively controlling of her daughter after Wowza's brother tragically died.

Her father, having been forced as a youth to swallow his dreams of dancing professionally in order to pursue a wage-earning job, learned at an early age to disassociate himself from his emotions.

He developed an intolerance for emotional outbursts of any kind and made it clear to Wowza that she was too homely to ever become a dancer. So Wowza learned how to repress her innately jubilant personality out of fear of being punished.

Her father prevented any expressive behavior by her, by striking her with the feared razor strap. Her body became rigid with fear, but she convinced herself that if she endured any pain that he inflicted on her, he would admire her for her bravery and be kinder to her. She so desired to be swept up in the arms of her father and receive his approval.

She was constantly traumatized by the emotional land mines exploding between her parents. She developed a horrific skin rash that soon took over her body and covered her face. She was constantly mocked by her peers at school as they yelled, *Look out, it's leper girl! Don't get too close, you'll catch it!*

Six months after the skin disease started, her left eye pulled into the left corner of her socket. The doctor prescribed thick, coke bottle glasses that added insult to injury. She became so self-conscious that she had trouble engaging in school.

Teachers concluded that she had a learning disability because she became stiff with fright when called upon at school. When her parents were alerted, her father scolded, *You-stupid girl, how can you be so dumb?*

Wowza found solace at the playground when she went off by herself and began imagining her life as an exciting adventure. She became a female Robin Hood in a stratosphere above the world, saving frightened and abandoned children and taking them to a magical place of wonders.

On her 11th birthday, Wowza's mom bought her a full-length mirror. *Mirrors were my enemy,* she adds. *I couldn't stand the sight of the ugly rash all over my body.*

One day, she had an impulse to put on a Halloween mask. She began to play out an ugly old character…she went into deep anguish seeing her likeness to this ugly creature in the mirror, and her body tightened into a death grip as she gasped for breath. Suddenly an impulse of air forced its way through her body as she felt the delicious surge of life moving through her as never before. She felt her body's innate will to live and it got her thinking.

One day, Wowza was alone in her house. With no parents around to edit her she decided to experiment by letting go of her inhibitions. She danced and made noise and contorted her body. She said to herself, *If I can't be a beautiful dancer as my father says, I'll be the world's greatest ugly dancer, something I'm really good at.*

She continued practicing her dance steps until one day her father walked in on her and cruelly mocked her. She felt deadened like a stone slab; tears welled up in her so severely she couldn't hold back the river of her emotions. To her amazement, for the first time, she felt the profound relief of her buried feelings.

As tears began to fall she desperately distracted herself from her emotions by gazing at a beautiful portrait on the wall which was described by her mother as 'The Mother of the World.' Mesmerized, Wowza began imagining The Mother of the World opening her arms to embrace her, comfort her and love her. She imagined that this mother hummed to her a comforting lullaby known to her as *The Hum of Love.*

From then on Wowza held close to her heart, her inner companion she called *Humma.* She began using *Humma,* as she hummed *The Hum of Love* in the morning, hummed to school and to sleep at night. She consoled herself from her parent's vindictive behavior toward her by beginning to imagine that they were actors in an outrageous play. She began to see everyone as part of her live cinema.

The itching of her skin became so unbearable that she looked in the mirror and screamed out her repressed self-hatred. She then consoled herself with *The Hum of Love* and felt strokes of compassion overtake her. Miraculously, by facing and giving voice to her shadow and replacing it with self-compassion, the itching and the rash began to disappear, and she began to heal. She got an operation for her crossed-eye, and day by day, she shape-shifted her life with the daily sounding of her inner companion, *Humma.*

Her spirits and self-confidence were on the rise. One sunny day she jubilantly ran down a hill to the beach and spread out her arms with sheer joy. A man walked up and took her picture. A popular holiday magazine soon boasted her photo with the caption, *Radiant Beauty under the Sun!*

This was a turning point in her life. From that photo, the cat was out of the bag. The ugly duckling had turned into a beautiful swan and she was the last to know. Her photo was discovered, and she was invited to enter a Miss Florida Gladiola pageant…and won! This cascaded into a series of high profile beauty pageants. She traveled as Spokeswoman for the Florida Citrus Industry, became a Good Will Ambassador for the State of Florida and appeared in over 100 radio and TV programs around the country. She became Miss Florida 1957 and a runner up at the Miss America Pageant.

Her love for music and theatre led her to study acting at the famed Actor's Studio under Lee Strasberg. She became an accomplished Hollywood actress and even acted alongside Marilyn Monroe and a number of other high-profile actors. She effortlessly shape-shifted her character into a multitude of roles from beauty to beast. She credits her dramatic range, largely to acting out her emotions in front of the mirror as a young child.

Wowza used the traumatic years of her youth as a springboard for creating an exciting life filled with a palate of rich experiences. She serves as an inspiration to others, showing that under one's traumatic history or physical disfigurements, there resides a loving compassionate presence within that can rise above it all. She's devoted her life to helping others see through the inhibitory barriers of guilt, shame and fear into reveling in the beauty and power of their essential nature.

For the last four decades Wowza has inspired individuals, actors and speakers as an expressive arts therapist and spent the 1970s as an acting teacher at Antioch College in LA. She went on to coaching and preparing guests for *The Johnny Carson Show* in the 80s. In the 90s she was creator and director of her own performing arts company, *Theatre of the Earth.*

Wowza also helped pioneer the human potential movement and collaborated with renowned leaders including Joseph Campbell and Gabrielle Roth. She developed *The Wowza Method*, teaching people how to integrate the body with breath, voice, movement, feelings and the brilliance of the mind. For the last ten years, she has taught *Expressive Arts for Performing Artists* and *Gestalt Therapy* in Mainland China.

As a dynamic and gorgeous 82-year old empowerment leader, Wowza teaches *Wowza's Ageless Energetics; The 7 Life-Force Processes; Busting Loose of the Aging Game; Wowzasize…*and most affectionately; *The Hum of Love!   To learn more:* https://wowzaagelessvitality.com

EMPOWERED WOMAN #3:

ELEANOR ROOSEVELT

The purpose of life is to live it, to taste experience to the utmost, to reach out eagerly and without fear for a newer and richer experience.
— Eleanor Roosevelt

It may be obvious by the multiple quotes I've included in this book, that I am an Eleanor Roosevelt fan. She was a woman who bridged the gap between partisan politics. She saw it and called it like it was and applied herself wholeheartedly to her stance for human dignity, regardless of a person's origin, gender, or political leanings.

Born October 11, 1884, in New York, Eleanor, the shy niece of President Theodore Roosevelt was born into a family of privilege. Her privilege turned to tragedy at the age of 10 when she found herself orphaned, sad and isolated.

Her mother, Anna, was known as one of New York's most stunning beauties. Anna was not always kind to her daughter, however. She made Eleanor deeply self-conscious about her homely appearance and serious demeanor. She labeled her 'granny' at a time when young Eleanor was burdened by her mother's declining health and ultimate demise. Remembering her childhood, Eleanor later wrote, *I was a solemn child without beauty. I seemed like a little old woman entirely lacking in the spontaneous joy and mirth of youth.*

Her larger than life father, Elliott, dominated Eleanor's memories. He adored her with his humor and charming, uncritical nature. However, her father's passion only underscored the isolation she felt when he was absent with his social affairs. He became extremely depressed by his wife's death, and later died of alcoholism.

Eleanor was sent to boarding school in England at age 14, which was a major turning point in her life. The headmistress of the school, Mademoiselle Marie Souvestre, was a bold and radical feminist whose drive was to educate her students to become leaders. Eleanor had the privilege of traveling with her head mistress who showed her both the grandeur and the squalor of various cultures. Early on, her path was stoic and mission-driven.

In 1905, she married her distant cousin, Franklin Delano Roosevelt. His mother's extreme disapproval of Eleanor was matched by her fervent attempt to break them up. They married however and gave birth to six children. At the same time Eleanor became active in public service, working for the American Red Cross during World War I.

While her husband was serving as assistant Naval Secretary during World War I, a rumor surfaced linking Franklin to an affair with his secretary. After finding love letters between them, and later discovering subsequent affairs, she considered leaving. She recognized, however, that her departure would end his political career and her ability to serve humanity on a larger scale.

After Franklin suffered a polio attack in 1921, Eleanor cared for him.

Despite some ideological differences she encouraged his return to politics. When Franklin became President in 1933, Eleanor dramatically changed the role of the First Lady. His disability somehow freed her to become more involved in political causes of her own.

Eleanor demonstrated to the world that the First Lady was an important part of American politics. Although she was highly criticized for her active role in public policy and continually ridiculed for her homely features, she was determined to break barriers and get things done.

She became involved with the League of Women Voters; she championed human rights, women's issues and children's issues. She also used her office to help the country's poor and bravely stood up against racial discrimination.

She pioneered the use of mass media by holding press conferences and even had her own newspaper to communicate directly with the public at a time when the country was coming out of the great depression.

During World War II, Eleanor traveled abroad to visit U.S. troops. After her husband's death in 1945, she was selected to be a delegate to the United Nations General Assembly, serving from 1945 to 1953. She further strengthened her legacy in her stand for human rights and became the chair of the UN's Human Rights Commission. As a part of this commission, she helped to write the Universal Declaration of Human Rights.

In addition to her political work, Eleanor wrote several books about her extraordinary life, including *This Is My Story* (1937), *This I Remember* (1949), *On My Own* (1958), and *Autobiography* (1961). During the same year her autobiography was published, she returned to public service. President Kennedy made her a delegate to the United Nations in 1961 and selected her to serve as chair of the Commission on the Status of Women.

A revolutionary first lady and audaciously empowered woman, she was one of the most outspoken women to ever live in the White House. Despite her critics, no one could contest her role as a great humanitarian who not only paved the way for human rights, but for women's liberation. She remained steadfast to her life purpose, leaving a rich legacy behind her while paving the way for the freedom of others.

CREATING A
NEW FOUNDATION

The word 'diva' to me means
doing something supernatural
with something natural.

—Patti Lupone

CHAPTER SIX
CREATING A
NEW FOUNDATION

One way we can measure our progress in terms of attracting healthy personal relationships, is by asking ourselves:

What is the quality of my relationship to myself? Do I love myself? Can I look myself in the mirror and appreciate my inherent beauty rather than the flaws?

Do I show up for myself in my actions, my eating habits, my exercise schedule, my conversations, the intonation of my voice, my self-expression?

Do I show it in my posture, the clothes I wear, the people I choose to align with? Do I honor myself by partaking in activities that align with my soul's passions?

It's helpful to periodically take a personal inventory and ask ourselves these questions with radical honesty. We can then highlight the attributes we're proud of and readjust the behaviors that demean us. When we focus on our positive attributes, our internal chemistry reverberates, and our inner radiance becomes palpable.

Self-respect is authenticity at its finest. It restores honor to life. As we live a life that is self-honoring and is honorable to others, we change the game of life. The daily practices we keep and the integrity in our relationships we cultivate reverberate out, profoundly impacting our immediate circle of influence as well as the world around us on a grander scale.

Life Assessment Check Sheet

Here's a helpful life assessment check sheet for reviewing where you are right now and determining where you'd like to be:

Who Am I?

- How do I see myself and what are my core values?
- What qualities do I exhibit that match my core values?
- What of my qualities fall short of my core values?
- What are the unique gifts I am bringing to the world?
- What are my passions and the things that give me joy?
- What activities in my life support my passions?
- What are my signature life statements that keep me on track?
- Am I a generous person or one who is withholding?
- Do I happily allow others to be generous to me?

What Stays and What Goes?

- Which of my lifestyle habits support me and which demean me?
- Which relationships in my life resonate with my core values?
- Which relationships drain my energies and distract me from my path?

Where Am I?

- What is the quality of my current living environment?
- What is the quality of my current work environment?
- What is the quality of my social environment?
- What is the quality of my internal environment or spiritual state?
- Which of these resonate with my soul's purpose and which do not?

Where Do I Want to Be?

- Am I measuring up to my higher potential?
- What areas in my life do I desire to improve upon?
- What aspects of myself still need healing?
- What action steps can I take to further heal?
- What is my commitment to myself for actualizing my chosen passions?

How Do I Get There?

- What roadblocks do I need to overcome to achieve the life of my dreams?
- Is my current living environment serving my highest good?
- Is my work environment aligned with my life's core purpose?
- Is my social environment loving and mutually supportive?
- Who are my role models and allies for success?
- What is my strategic plan for moving my life forward in a significant way?

- How am I practicing love and forgiveness?
- What am I modeling in my life that is attracting my desired outcomes?

What are My Action Steps?

- What are my non-negotiable core principles that serve as my guideposts?
- What action steps can I take right now to bring me closer to my dreams?
- Who are my conscious collaborators, and accountability partners?
- What system do I have in place to measure my continued progress?
- What are my success mantras in the face of adversity?
- Do I recognize and reward my wins, great and small?
- How do I celebrate my wins? Do I include others in the fun?
- How do I recognize and support the wins of others?

Once we've answered these questions for ourselves, it's time to take decisive action. Even if some of our action plans have unexpected outcomes we can continue to assess, adjust and move forward in the direction of our dreams.

We've all learned by now to expect the unexpected in life. Change is life's guarantee. The key for each of us is not to let life's curveballs derail us from our path. As unforeseen circumstances arise, fluidity of thought, accompanied by humor and present-time affirmative action helps us to maintain our equilibrium.

Creative Solution-Finders

One of the most empowering actions we can employ is the act of becoming creative solution finders. Creative solution solving overrides the victimized state of being part of the problem, and instead moves us, and others, into a progressive place where miraculous resolutions can occur. We become powerful co-collaborators of new-possibility thinking.

Great mastery can be achieved when we take a problem or a difficult relationship and transform it into a grand new design. If others are determined to rain on our parade, we can simply move on, laugh it off and hold our head high. Liberation comes when we look above and beyond a situation rather than staying stuck in the mud.

Expanding Our Containers

We can travel abroad and explore the many wonders of the world, yet many of us have been living in a very small container emotionally. As we broaden our and expand our world view with greater curiosity, understanding and compassion, we develop a broader aptitude for interacting with others and defining our unique place in this world.

Increasingly, souls are creating "enlightened entrepreneurism" by developing their passions into viable businesses, making a valuable contribution to others, and experiencing deep fulfillment in the process.

The timeless quest for "the soul to be free" has been fought and forged by counter-culture revolutionaries throughout time. God bless the revolutionaries. God bless the true pioneers of our freedoms. Let's insure that their efforts have not been in vain.

If you are unsure what to do in your life, simply listen to your heart and ask what the world needs of you. Dare to dream, and bravely move in the direction of your dreams.

In this never-before pivotal moment in history, the path has been painstakingly paved before us. Plant the seeds of your potential into the earth. Support their growth with your passionate dedication, harvest them and bring them into their natural fulfillment.

SELF-LOVE RITUAL

Connecting with Your Tree of Life

Clearly, our daily tasks and experiences become more productive when we're grounded. Likewise, our activities become more meaningful by our connection to Spirit. In between these two connections lies the nexus of consciousness that bridges Heaven and Earth from within, as we operate in the world of form.

Consider that your life is like a Mighty Tree.

Take a moment to stand barefoot on the ground. Visualize invisible roots beneath your feet, firmly grounding you in Mother Earth. You are continually nourished by the depth and breadth of her natural resources. As you branch yourself upward for guidance and inspiration, you open yourself to the wisdom of the universe, and the music of creation ignites your passions.

You stand stronger each passing year, as concentric rings of wisdom (like rings around a tree trunk) strengthen your core, widen your perspective and deepen your magnetic field of attraction. Your energy brings tranquility to the human landscape around you.

As the seasons and storms of life come and go, you stand and sway, knowing that your light source is ever present, even amidst the darkest of days. Your breath receives and releases life force as an atmospheric dance, that igniting your interplay with all of life.

Your buds and blossoms bring the inspiration of new beginnings. In full bloom, you shelter and shade souls on their journey while you hold court with the sun and the moon and the stars. The fruit of your actions bring the sweet message of a cycle well-fulfilled.

*We must be willing to get rid of the life
we've planned, so as to have the life
that is waiting for us. The old skin has
to be shed before the new one can come.*

--Joseph Campbell

CHAPTER SEVEN
SELF-REFERRED LOVE

*One can never consent to creep
when one feels an impulse to soar.*

— Helen Keller

CHAPTER SEVEN
SELF-REFERRED LOVE

Each of us as women has been born with a core essence that makes us special. It's our job to continually reinforce the qualities of our essence in our life practices so they become a natural expression of who we are. This requires us to live and move with a higher vision.

Have you ever created a vision board that is filled with pictures and affirmative statements you desire to attract in your life? Well, in essence, our entire life should be treated as a vision board. The arrangement of items and the experiences you chose for your home, your car and your workplace...as well as the role you choose for your life become your personal template.

Vision vs. Attachment

Occasionally, we may attach our self-worth to the roles in life we play and to the notions of the way life should be. Because change is inevitable and is not always within our control, our notions may be challenged, pushing us beyond our comfort zones.

Over-identification with our roles can cause a false sense of security, or even a vacant sense of self-worth. Embracing change and choosing the way we respond, empowers us to seize the opportunity for growth and find peace within the yet unknown terrain of our lives. Retaining the vision of our dreams is the life raft that keeps us moving forward no matter what and gives us emotional equilibrium.

Self-compassion combined with with vision helps us continuously 'fill our own cup' throughout our life sojourn and gives us a strong internal core that holds us together when the shit hits the fan.

We live in a culture that popularizes flawlessness and aggressively promotes women as sex objects. We find ourselves under immense pressure to become a flawless external package, distracting us from cultivating our inherent beauty from within.

Striving to measure up to the touched-up magazine models of today, we may find ourselves becoming discouraged as we give power to our imagined flaws rather than our fabulous virtues.

These imagined flaws could be our body's saddle bags rather than smooth thighs; a large nose rather than a petite one or small breasts rather than large ones. The list goes on and on. These then, become the silent messages that energetically broadcast: *I'm not good enough to be loved, valued or admired because of these flaws,* regardless of all manner of external measures to cover them up.

There's nothing wrong with enhancing our beauty if it is born of self-love. In fact, a woman's attendance to her outer appearance exemplifies self-care. It's sexy and desirable. The most attractive women, however, first cultivate beauty on the inside which then radiates on the outside.

The quality that makes all women wildly attractive above and beyond all outer appearances is…attitude! A woman's attitude, her alignment with her inner beauty and her passionate pursuit of her life purpose is undeniably seductive.

The divas of this world have an interesting handle on this. They carry within them, an attitude that says, *I'm 'All That' and don't even try to tell me different!* They have developed a set of internal laws that state: *This is who I AM…you will know me by my special signature.*

The divas know that it's not what you <u>have</u> that makes you interesting. It's what you <u>do</u> with what you have.

There's no better time than now to upgrade this archetype by becoming a divine diva--a woman who embodies the confidence of a diva tempered by the qualities of compassion, humility and generosity. The world needs women who exemplify the new standard of feminine power!

As women, we have every right to be blissfully unapologetic for living out our lives as our magnificent selves. This principle is at the core of self-love.

We have no time to waste with the endless ruminations of the old wounded self. It's time to be bold, brave and powerfully feminine. It is time to shine with our life purpose and to mature it into absolute fulfillment. The world awaits the gift of each woman.

As empowered women we must ask ourselves:

What is my unique signature that I have come here to create? How do I paint this signature upon the canvas of time, and how does it inspire others along the way?

Signature Life Statements

> *Don't wait for a light to appear at the end of the tunnel.*
> *Stride down there and light the bloody thing yourself.*
> — *Sara Henderson*

The empowered woman defines for herself, her signature life statements. In other words, the philosophical messages she lives by make her uncompromisingly happy and proud to be who she is.

She defines for herself what her life messages are that will illuminate a world dampened by cynicism. She designs her solution-mantras that speak to unforeseen circumstances and keep her from derailment, thus reinforcing her resilience.

So, whatever our signature life statements are, it's helpful to keep in mind that no matter what the circumstance, we are experiencing the dynamics of our own life theater that to a large degree, we have chosen to participate in. The key here is to choose authenticity in every moment and refer to our core values as we play out our role as fabulous divine divas.

As we gain forward momentum in embodying our signature life statements we can more positively impact unforeseen circumstances and perhaps even avert negative situations before they have a chance to get out of the gate.

Our lives must include a bit of pliability, especially when it comes to the undependable nature of human relationships. We can take a lesson from the trees and stand strong and sway with life's storms.

As we embrace this paradox within our world, we will find ourselves less attached and less disappointed in life's outcome and instead become more appreciative of the journey.

Eliminating the 'Should-ster'

Who is a 'should-ster?" You know, those of us who use the word "should" to drive our behaviors. The 'shoulds' such as, *I should do this, you should do that, I should have done this, you should have done that,* are those pesky expectations brought on by fear that often do nothing more than create entrapment.

This statement is not to negate the fact that we, as a society, have come to expect behaviors of basic human respect toward one another, and conduct that insures our safety and sovereignty.

Rather, the 'shoulds' are those constricting expectations we may occasionally impose upon ourselves and others in order to control an outcome. A controlled outcome rarely unfolds as expected. It commonly results in stress and discord because the outcome of not meeting the expectations are often met with guilt and shame.

No one can control the behavior of others. We can, however, choose the nature of our own behavior in the face of circumstances. We can contribute to a positive outcome, even if it means a change of plans or an unexpected redefinition of certain relationships.

As we learn how to overcome the need for control and instead become empowered feminine communicators and creative solution finders, we bring the quality of enchantment into a given situation. This approach influences human behavior on an entirely different level. Enchantment elevates the spirit as an alchemy of sorts, to bring out the best in everyone involved.

The art of enchantment is an ancient, heart-centered life skill that requires conscientious practice. Enchantment is an earnest intention of inspiring a positive full-circle response to a given situation. It is the higher path over using one's charm, agenda or forcefulness to control or manipulate an end result.

Morning Signature Life Statements

When we wake up in the morning, we each have the opportunity for positively setting the tone of our day. I like to wake in the morning with this signature life statement:

I am alive to live a day of greatness! Welcome life, welcome love, welcome natural solutions for my health and wholeness! Welcome divine appointments! Welcome creative solutions! Welcome collaborative enterprise, moving my life forward in the direction of my dreams! Welcome souls to my heart, with whom I may share love and be of service to this day!

By expressing these types of signature life statements in present time, we're setting the stage and building a momentum for good things to come. It also helps us gain stability and become less derailed in the face of unpredictable circumstances as they occur.

We begin to recognize that we are taking our positive energy and plowing through the field of collective consciousness shrouded by an old encrusted world order. We begin planting positive seeds within ourselves and others that ignite standards of excellence for joyful and enlightened living.

What a pivotal moment in time it is to be alive.

Soulful Contemplation Before Sleep

A great way to set the tone for the evening is by writing the wins of the day in a journal, as well as things we're burdened by. Recording our burdens followed by written, positive affirmations releases negativity from our minds during sleep, and replaces it with seeds of divine potential into our waking consciousness.

Avoiding television programming a couple of hours before retiring helps us to go to sleep with our own thoughts and inspirations, rather than becoming receptacles for the subliminal projections of media programming. Negative media programming can create psychic unrest in our subconscious during sleep.

Meditation, deep breathing and soulful contemplation before sleep help us to remove the stresses held in by the body and more easily moves our soul into divine realms. We can pray to be shown on inner levels, a grander vision for our lives than we currently hold, and for remembrance of this vision upon awakening.

Embracing Our Sexuality

A woman's sexuality is her treasure chest. It is a sacred gateway to divine love and consciousness. The key for us is to retain or regain our juicy essence by using our sexuality in many wise and creative ways by the way we move, speak and express our being.

Sexuality and creativity are intrinsically linked. They are laced as an ancient tenet of primal power and artistic expression that is evidenced in every culture throughout history.

The sexual act itself plays out as a primal dance of creation, as the masculine and feminine energies become one. This is why it's so important for women to choose wisely when it comes to our sexual exchanges with a partner. Our sexual fluids are the nectars that blend together and become part of our interior terrain.

These fluids can provide the exchange of nourishment and feelings of bliss when the qualities of love, care and respect are in the mix.

While spontaneous sex with a new partner can be extremely erotic and fulfilling, a woman must use discernment to safeguard herself from taking in a partner's energies and fluids that she might later regret. Women, by the nature of being feminine receivers, are the receptacles of a man's fluids and the quality of consciousness retained in those fluids, whether we use contraceptives or not.

Likewise, we give of ourselves in ways that our masculine counterpart hungers for. We give the nectar of our innermost sacred self, which is why it's such a natural act for us to bond after sex. Our souls can easily, energetically create a tryst with someone, because within the exchange of fluids, are the subtle messengers or the codes of the partner's life story.

Many of us do not yet have the discernment when it comes to taking in our partner's codes, and the tryst that's created after a sexual exchange can be difficult to shake. It can sometimes become traumatic if and when the relationship doesn't work out.

As an empowered woman, it's important to recognize that each of us is a goddess who has the power to choose. We must listen to our innermost sacred self who instinctively knows whether or not a sexual exchange with someone is in resonance with our soul's higher purpose.

Even when we are not in a sexual partnership, we can fulfill the desires of our innermost being by loving and nurturing our own bodies and using the power of our creativity in every aspect of our lives. Beauty itself is born out of love's creative act between the heaven and earth. Nature itself, in all of its grandeur, is the great example of the intelligent exchange of primal power and artistic expression.

SELF-LOVE RITUAL

Creating a Love Banquet

Think of your life as a love banquet, always ready to be filled with a colorful palate of experiences.

You are the host of the love banquet. You are continuously preparing delicious experiences for yourself and those who you chose to engage with. You welcome your chosen guests into your life to dine with the divine, share the elixir of love and savor meaningful conversation.

You can take this ritual into the physical realm and create artful experiences that stir the ancient memory of the grand goddess within you.

Try this:

Collect an aromatic array of organic fresh fruits, vegetables, flowers and herbs from your garden or the local farmers market. Bring your treasures of nature into your kitchen.

Live in the moment as you stand in your kitchen with expanded mindfulness and full sensory experience. Open your awareness to the scent of your fresh delights, their texture and their beauty. Prepare yourself for a feast.

Invite others beforehand or in the spur of the moment to partake in your banquet experience. Relish each stage of your artistic ritual as you welcome your guests to clean, chop, cook, invent and prepare the setting with you. Then to celebrate as if you are preparing for royalty – which is all of you!

Ask yourselves, "What is the most delicious, inventive and healthy concoction we can prepare right now to take our vitality to the next level?"

Allow your collective genius and your senses to be your guide. Include fresh aromatic herbs and edible flowers in your creation. Use delicious cold-pressed olive oil, walnut oil, sesame oil and/or ghee to anoint your food with its golden goodness. Enhance your culinary experience with raw toasted nuts, seeds, fresh garlic, onion, tasty medicinal mushrooms and peppers.

Add your favorite music to your ritual. Sing and move to the music barefooted. Feel the texture of the floor beneath you as you spice up your culinary delight. Dress in your favorite goddess wear and be sexy, spicy...and as delectable as your food!

Set your table with fresh flowers, candles, freshly made aromatic condiments, colorful dishes, napkins and glassware.

Creatively invent new recipes of freshly prepared elixirs such as infusing sparkling water with a few drops of edible aromatic essential oils. Or, adding fresh pomegranate and grapefruit juices together and topping it off with a splash of sparkling water and a twig of mint. Or, steeping fresh rosemary twigs in hot water and adding natural orange flavored honey. The possibilities are endless!

You may choose to add fine organic wines or naturally flavored libations to your experience. I suggest you also try celebrating your sensory experience free of alcohol and discover new ways to give yourself a natural high. You may find that it will not only heighten your senses but will sweeten your body's internal chemistry and leave you clear headed in the morning!

Excite your palate with nature-made desserts such as fresh seasonal fruits, raw honey, fresh cinnamon, ginger, goat/ sheep yogurts, cheeses and coconut—all of which aid in digestion and leave you feeling satisfied.

Allow the atmosphere to take on a life of its own by delighting together in the smells and tastes of your co-creation. Initiate uplifting conversation and remember to bring some humor into the mix! There's nothing better after a meal than a good belly-laugh over life's absurdities.

One of the most insightful experiences I've had at a dinner party was when each of us expressed three words that positively described the special essence we saw in one another. When my turn came around, I was astounded at the perceptions others had of me! It got me thinking how powerfully we broadcast ourselves in ways we may not be fully aware of, as well as how meaningful the encouraging words of others are.

Why not enjoy cleaning up together, making the experience as fun and humor-filled as the rest of your banquet? The ritual of togetherness is what memories are made of, which in turn, invites more of the same!

People are like stained-glass windows.
They sparkle and shine when the sun
is out, but when the darkness sets in,
their true beauty is revealed only if
there is light from within.

-— Elisabeth Kübler-Ross

CHAPTER EIGHT

EMBODYING THE EMPOWERED PATH

Just think of all
those women on the Titanic
who said, 'No, thank you'
to dessert that night.
And for what?

— Erma Bombeck

CHAPTER EIGHT
EMBODYING THE EMPOWERED PATH

As emerging heroines, we can find inspiration from those who have paved the way before us and have set a personal course of action that exemplifies empowered living at its finest.

We know the empowered woman by her practices. We now have an opportunity to model these practices with greater understanding complimented by our personal life signature.

Put these ideas on for size:

SELF-LOVE RITUAL

Modeling the Self-Made Woman

Dare to Be a Bit Outrageous

There's nothing more exciting than an adventurous women--one who says *Yes!* to life's opportunities when they come knocking at her door.

Appreciate each moment as if it was your last and be purposeful in creating a life filled with meaningful moments. As you expand your powers of perception, you can even find humor in life's challenging and illogical moments and avoid taking yourself too seriously. Just when you think you're all composed, life may give you a piece of humble pie. *So why not add some whip cream?!*

In other words, a bit of humor can get you out the stickiest of situations. The audacity to be great, funny and spontaneous in the face of what might have formerly been perceived to be an embarrassment opens the door to a more enchanting life.

Be Gutsy in the Face of Adversity

As an empowered, self-made woman, season your life with adventure by excelling beyond your perceived abilities. Become impervious to the negative labeling and the imposed opinions by others of your perceived limitations. Persevere.

Live in excitement, knowing you are a passionate pioneer who embodies excellence and the audacious power of the human spirit. Take calculated risks and trust your instincts, rather than taking careless risks. View any setbacks as valuable data for recalibrating your course onto the right track.

Take Excellent Care of Your Health

Enhance your health with a variety of personal care practices that ensure your ability to move through life with optimal health.

Rise each day by alkalizing your body with pure water and a fresh squeeze of lemon or a spoonful of apple cider vinegar. These allow your body to flush out toxins and balance out your Ph level.

Nourish your body with fresh organic superfoods such as berries in season, fresh greens, medicinal mushrooms and other phytonutrients. These nutrients are fortified to super-charge your body with vital life force and support your endocrine system during the various stages of your life. Consult your local health food outlets for suggestions.

Collaborate with qualified professionals who incorporate a holistic approach to your health. Become an avid investigator of ground-breaking innovations for maintaining optimum health—those that harmonize with your body draw upon the world's natural resources.

Maintain fluidity in your body by constantly moving your body. Enhance your core strength as outlined in this book and expand your body's flexibility. Keep your mind agile and stimulated while organizing and simplifying your life to minimize stress.

When stressful circumstances are unavoidable, remember to breathe deeply and exhale the tension out of your body. Shake it off! Uplift your psyche and your soul with music, song and positive affirmations to keep yourself in a positive, empowered state.

Consume foods that harmonize with the seasons and synergize with your cultural background. Eating in harmony with the rhythmic cycles of the sun can also maximize your body's health.

Supercharge your body with fresh fruits, vegetables, superfoods and protein foods upon rising; then again, at noon when the sun is highest in the sky to maximize digestion and assimilation; followed by a lighter meal at sunset before retiring.

The body is in repair and restoration during sleep, so it's helpful to avoid heavy, hard-to-digest foods in the evening.

Become a Spa Ritualist

How rewarding it is to continually self-nurture. Enchant your body and spirit by creating a lovely home spa.

Cleanse, exfoliate and mask your face with nature's finest ingredients. Enliven your scalp and your neurons with an invigorating scalp massage. Lovingly and consciously groom your hair – think of your locks as a physical extension of your brain waves.

Take excellent care of your hands and feet as they contain thousands of nerve endings that correspond to every organ in your body. Comfort your body with pure essential oil products, nourishing organic lotions and body butters. Infuse the air with scented candles, fragrant flowers and music. Sip herbal elixirs during your home spa ritual that soothe and calm your senses.

Allow yourself to be pampered by others as well, by receiving spa treatments as a part of your sensuous life practice.

Dare to Dream and Fulfill Your Dreams

Take fearless, decisive action in the direction of your dreams. Measure yourself to a divine standard rather than measuring yourself according to the imposed standards of others. Eleanor Roosevelt once said: *What you think of me is none of my business.*

Celebrate your wins, great and small, and celebrate the wins of others with equal joy as if they were your own!

The only limit a woman actually has is her ability to hold a grander vision for her life, and her confidence to pursue it. Use your imagination, your eye-magic-in-action to in-vision solutions in an honorable way for yourself and others.

You can journal, create a vision board and an action plan for achieving your goals, and then engage your passions into it. As a creative alchemist you have myriad of options for renewing your life path. Dedicate yourself to its fulfillment and reflect upon your progress along the way.

Be unafraid to reinvent yourself and change your life story if you are inspired to do so, or if your life is moving in the wrong direction. If your personal direction is better served by a re-evaluation and life adjustment, go for it!

> *The most creative minds can take any circumstance,*
> *problem or misstep and use it as a springboard for*
> *birthing a whole new paradigm.*
> — *Christina*

Champion a Cause Greater Than Yourself

As you refine your empowerment skills you will soon become a success magnet. You can then use your successes to give back to others. Align your talents and your efforts toward a path that resonates with your soul. Recognize that the peaks and valleys of your soul's journey need not be in vain so long as you share the fruit of your life lessons with others who are in the process of discovery.

If you follow your heart, if you listen to your gut, and if you extend
your hand to help another, not for any agenda, but for the sake of
humanity, you are going to find the truth.
— *Erin Brockovich*

As you are in a perpetual state of self-discovery, recognize that as you serve, you're operating from a level playing field with your acquaintances, loved ones and those struggling along the way.

Educate Yourself Continuously

Continuously upgrade your own internal software by educating yourself in areas that compliment your interests. Gain an appetite for learning! Expand your areas of expertise to build confidence on a personal and professional level and expand your ability to be of greater service.

Avoid stagnation. Allow yourself to be taught by your contemporaries even when you perceive yourself to be an expert. Your ability to be agile in your thinking rather than prideful allows for a greater flow of resourcefulness and collaboration.

If and when you find yourself challenged by a contemporary's one-upmanship, devise a way to compliment the competitor with a brilliant statement or action that dissipates the energy...all-the-while showing a spirit of cooperation that underlies a message that you are too expansive for such nonsense.

Use each life experience as a springboard for your soul's evolution. Craft your lessons as an offering for the betterment of others. Uphold an attitude of gratitude. Shape-shift your world to be a grand adventure of the highest order.

Be Beautiful from the Inside Out

You are born of love. You are made in the image of all things beautiful and you have all the resources to resonate beauty from your core. Become a lover of nature and bring nature's beauty into your daily life practices.

Be a delicious and juicy creature! Exude passion and purpose! Incorporate art and music into your daily life. Create, cook, sing and dance with wild abandon! You have the ability to divine yourself as an elegant goddess while being equally beguiling as a tomboy. Love your multi-dimensional self in all of its expressions.

We are experiencing the newly emerging community of "woman code." It represents the rise of the ancient feminine goddess within us all that serves as a non-dualistic force for good.

The phoenix goddess is rising from the ashes and brings with her, the evolution of a soul who has been through the refiner's fire and lives to merge what once was divided.

The act of "bonding" amongst women, bonding with our children and with our mates is not just an emotional and psychological phenomenon. It's chemical.

As we spoke of earlier, the act of bonding through loving relationships produces an entire chemical "cocktail" that generates a magnetic field of positive and desirable qualities around a woman, far surpassing the altered 'feel good' effects of any liquid libation.

Medical science reveals that there is a correlation between bonding and a woman's oxytocin and progesterone levels which tends to increase her levels of happiness and make her even more sexy.

Thus, a woman's primal need to have close and intimate communications is an intuitive and instinctual act – the benefits of which can be far reaching.

It starts with self-love.

So, let's live our lives as a grand ritual and demonstrate within us, the highest levels of self-love. In turn we become more lovable to others and draw healthy love relationships into our lives.

Let's love our men and delight in showing it. As we resist the temptation to generalize or negatively categorize the nature of men, we will instead allow a man to reveal himself to us as an individual, all-the-while maintaining our self-discernment.

Let's celebrate the women in our lives as sacred sisters rather than competitors. We honor them as co-creative partners of feminine expression and transformational love.

CHAPTER NINE
BECOMING CHANGE AGENTS

Remember, if you ever
need a helping hand,
you'll find one at the
end of your arm.
As you grow older
you will discover
that you have two hands —
one for helping yourself,
the other for helping others.

— Audrey Hepburn

CHAPTER NINE
BECOMING
CHANGE AGENTS

A new imperative for women is on the rise...

Women all over the world are responding to a deep, inner-prompting to become powerful change agents and pave the way for a world of enlightened living. It's our time, as women, to reawaken our inner genius as never before. It's our time to bring our feminine medicine into a world seeking a way for living more peacefully and honorably.

Creatures of the natural world are innately connected to universal intelligence. There is a special language in nature that enlivens a woman's ancient intuitive connection to this primordial sacred energy. It is within this nurturing relationship that she co-exists as a being of universal intelligence in a human body, whose purpose is to bring the human experience into the light.

The Sacred Codes Upon Our Path

This is a moment of all moments to be alive as women and to be engaged in the process. The old human order is literally crumbling beneath our feet, only to reveal the sacred codes upon our path which integrate colors, sounds, scents, vibrations and cosmic intelligence that are increasingly transforming our global community.

The long-awaited 2012 Venus transit across the sun continues to be celebrated by astrologers and philosophers as a catalyst for the rise of feminine energy into leadership.

What does this mean to us, as women today? It's to design new careers that draw upon our innate talents as visionaries, leaders and peacemakers sourced from the divine blueprint we were born with.

Just as we began this voyage as a spark of creation into a tiny embryo, it is my hope that these pages have inspired each of you to be brave in your expedition toward becoming a magnificent and empowered, self-made woman.

As you do, you will help to nurture the embryonic state of human evolution as we depart from the worn old paradigm of 'business as usual.' Let's be at peace, dear sisters, in moments when we feel suspended in the space between the lines. We've been gestating new life formulas for the soul of humanity.

Together, we're giving birth to a more conscious, collaborative community whose diversity is seen as part of the whole. We are part of a mass awakening of the female principle within us all, where unification (rather than the illusion of separation) is the order of the day.

As change agents, we're called to champion other women in pursuit of their dreams that, until now, they dared not reveal. Let's hold a higher standard by which we collaborate together as women, as well as with men.

Together, we can help one another discover our most powerful internal resources so we can all bring our unique gifts forward. The old model of competition is swiftly giving way to conscious collaboration. We are setting a new standard in the world on how relationship is done.

Above all, we have the supreme privilege of helping those who are struggling to get on their feet, and to teach souls how to become more chemically balanced so they can be less dependent upon anti-depressants. Let's continue to introduce holistic practices and the intuitive sciences into the mainstream so we can assist one another in becoming empowered rather than hopeless.

Let's be present and available for life's unexpected moments. Daily, we may find ourselves entertaining angels, unaware of the impact we can make in the lives of others, and their impact upon us. Please enjoy the story that accompanies this ritual:

SELF-LOVE RITUAL

Becoming a Present Time Blessing

Our lives unfold as a series of opportunities to discover the gift of each moment and to share our gifts with others in ways that serve and inspire them.

In those moments when you may be feeling small or unimportant, refresh yourself, renew your outlook, and be present for an opportunity to give. Appreciate how far you've come and recognize that there are others who are less fortunate than you who can benefit from your wisdom and kindness.

If you allow yourself to live fully in the present moment it will present to you, a divine appointment whereby you can extend yourself in a helpful way toward others.

A caring look, a thoughtful gesture, a kind word, an unexpected offering from you along with other acts of kindness are so powerful...they can literally save a life.

One day I was selecting breakfast from a grocery store food bar in downtown Los Angeles. I was approached by a very clean, well-dressed woman. She introduced herself as Kisha.

She began sharing with me her observance that the food bar wasn't very fresh and suggested that I consider another food bar down the street. Her overture opened up a remarkable conversation between us about her life.

Kisha practices yoga and lives on skid row. After hitting hard times, and being an unconventional person, she struggled to attend to her levels of self-care. She found herself continually rejected and prejudiced against for her unusual circumstances as she strived to secure a job and a wholesome living environment. The drug-infested community she lived in did not celebrate her for who she was in her heart. She had no kindred spirits to share herself with, so she found it difficult to carry on.

In her dignity, she never asked me for anything. I bought her breakfast and we continued a meaningful conversation. I told her how beautiful she was, and how much I admired her for how well she took care of herself amidst grueling conditions. We exchanged ideas, I offered her some help and I witnessed a ray of hope overshadow her. I could see that in a shining moment, her soul felt seen, validated...and valued.

I held Kisha in a field of love as I expressed appreciation for her beautiful heart. I shared with her, that she too can be an inspiration for others on skid row who are desperately seeking her wisdom. We said a prayer together, and she began to feel that her life had purpose.

I told her that I had to go to an appointment, so we began saying our good-byes. Before we departed she told me, *I was walking around the corner before entering this store, deciding if I was going to kill myself or not. You saved my life, thank you.*

We hugged as two souls on life's journey merging into one heart. There was no sense of separation or judgment. The presence of love literally transformed us both. I will never forget as I walked away, we held a long gaze, waved and smiled until we were out of each other's sight.

I clearly experienced a divine appointment. I was so grateful to be undeniably in the present moment to avail myself to a sister on the path. Unknowingly, I became a life-saver—an experience from which I will never be the same.

In the chaos and uncertainty of our current times, we have the opportunity to increase our bandwidth for living a life of magic and miracles, and to become change agents to a world in peril. We are each given guidance and support according to our ability to identify opportunity, call it forth, and welcome its bounty into our lives.

Each of us is an important agent for change. I invite you to recognize and embrace our life encounters as divine appointments. We need only champion the vital part we each play, as we reach out and touch the lives of others, infused with purpose stemming from deep levels of self-love.

Lend your voices only to sounds of freedom. No longer lend your strength to that which you wish to be free from. Fill your lives with love and bravery... and you shall lead a 'life uncommon.'

— Jewell

APPENDIX

SELF-LOVE
A WOMAN'S BOOK OF HEALING AND INSPIRATION

KEY CONCEPTS

Chapter One
Healing the Broken Heart

- Inherently, each of us is a divine masterpiece, holding within ourselves an exquisite original design of our full potential self.

- Many of us have found ourselves in embodiment shock and have become largely forgetful of our core identity and our prior sublime existence.

- Our current life span may have become tainted over the years from experiencing confusion with the undependable nature of human behavior.

- We may have become broken-hearted for being unseen and uncelebrated for who we truly are and the unique purpose for which we came into this world.

- We must dispel the myth that we, as women, have to be long-suffering in order to achieve approval or even love and fulfillment.

- We must cultivate new emotional associations to our life experiences, infusing us with self-compassion and the courage to forge new healthy pathways.

KEY CONCEPTS

Chapter Two
Shape-Shifting Our Beliefs

- In order for us to shape-shift our beliefs and associated emotions, it's helpful to get in touch with the core wounds we've accumulated during the early stages of our lives.

- This is a moment when we can become aware of the vibrations we've been carrying around, perhaps for our entire lives, or beyond — not knowing the keys that will set us free.

- We must learn to employ effective tools for embracing our emotions in order to enhance self-realization and communication with others.

- Meditation and contemplation bridge our outer awareness into our inner terrain. By sounding out the repressed emotions, we can release them from our cellular holding patterns, allowing us to externalize the pain of our layered wounds.

- The water content within each of us serves as an internal record keeper— a magnetic field of our emotionally charged beliefs. As we transform our beliefs, we change the vibration of the water in our cells and transform our electromagnetic field.

- Daily reinforcing positive self-talk with personal affirmations and actions will support new, empowering behavior.

KEY CONCEPTS

Chapter Three
Rewarding the Heroine

- We, as women are heroic beings. We give of ourselves so that others may thrive, often at the expense of our own well-being.

- The new paradigm of the empowered woman emphasizes high levels of self-expression and self-fulfillment, moving us into a juicier place of thriving rather than surviving.

- Let's align ourselves with peers who have cultivated wholesome relationships within themselves and have set their course in a direction that supports the success of others.

- 'The heroine's journey' as outlined in this book provides an interpretive window into the universal voyage for the empowered woman of today.

- As we accept accountability for our life circumstances we are saying to the universe: *I recognize how truly powerful I AM. I can take this same essential energy to reshape my life, beginning by establishing a new set of beliefs and subsequent actions.*

KEY CONCEPTS

Chapter Four
Reclaiming Our Birthright

- As emerging empowered women, it's essential to establish a healthy balance between our relationship with the facets of modern technology and our personal relationships with humans, animals and nature.

- Recognize that no matter what violations have pierced our life experiences, no one or no-thing can touch the original joy that resides within the soul.

- Recognizing our co-creative relationship with God and the unlimited universal power available to us generates momentum for attracting positive results and transforms our cellular magnetism.

- When we find ourselves impacted by the behavior of others, it's important to keep in mind that other people are also living their lives according to their own acquired internal laws.

- Detaching our emotions from a reactive response to the behavior of others frees our energies from unwholesome entanglement and gives us the resources to be creative solution finders.

KEY CONCEPTS

Chapter Five
Learning from Seasoned, Empowered Women
(Re-read the stories for your inspiration!)

Empowered Woman #1: Kathy Buckley:
At the end of your day, shake off the labels you wore of being a mom,
career woman, wife...or those pesky labels that say I'm not good enough.
Take a bath. Soak into the essence of
Who you truly are and revel in it!

Empowered Woman #2: Wowza:
All of life is vibrating and it's all humming! Every atom and particle in
the solar system is humming its own resonant tone. Call it God, spirit,
divinity, or wholeness; the truth is in the tone.

Empowered Woman #1: Eleanor Roosevelt
The purpose of life is to live it, to taste experience to
the utmost, to reach out eagerly and without fear for
a newer and richer experience.

KEY CONCEPTS

Chapter Six
Creating a New Foundation

- It's helpful to periodically take an internal inventory and ask ourselves questions to assess where we are with radical honesty. (Refer to the Life Assessment Check Sheet in this chapter.)

- Self-respect and self-honor exhibits authenticity at its finest.

- Change is life's guarantee. The key for each of us is not to let life's curveballs derail us from our path.

- One of the most empowering actions we, as women, can employ is the act of becoming creative solution-finders.

- Great mastery can be achieved when we take a problem or a difficult relationship and transform it into a grand new design.

KEY CONCEPTS

Chapter Seven
Self-Referred Love

- As we continually affirm with our highest qualities, we can embody a powerful new set of internal laws to live by.

- When we practice self-referred love and are continuously filling our own cup as we go through life, we have a strong internal core that holds us together when the shit hits the fan.

- As women, we have every right to become blissfully unapologetic for being our magnificent selves. This is the core of self-love.

- An empowered woman defines for herself signature life statements, the philosophical messages she lives by that make her uncompromisingly happy and proud to be who she is.

- We become even more masterful when we can blend our core values with pliability, especially when it comes to the undependable nature of human relationships. We can take a lesson from the trees and stand strong and sway with life's storms.

- The art of enchantment is a heart-centered life skill that requires conscientious practice. Enchantment is the intention of inspiring a positive full-circle response to a given situation. It is the higher path over using one's charm or agenda to control or manipulate an end result.

KEY CONCEPTS

Chapter Eight
Modeling the Self-Made Woman

- We know the self-made woman by her practices. We have the stellar opportunity to model these practices with renewed understanding and compliment them with our own unique life signature.

- Let's dare to be a little outrageous and be purposeful in creating a life filled with meaningful moments. Finding humor in life's absurdities will help us avoid taking ourselves too seriously.

- Being gutsy in the face of adversity seasons our lives with adventure by excelling beyond our perceived abilities.

- Let's persevere and become impervious to the negative labeling and the imposed opinions by others of our perceived limitations.

- As we fearlessly take decisive action in the direction of our dreams, we can celebrate our wins, great and small, and celebrate the wins of others with equal joy as if they were our own!

- Let's champion a cause greater than ourselves. As we continue to develop skills for becoming a success magnet we can use our successes to give back to others.

KEY CONCEPTS

Chapter Nine
Becoming a Change Agent

- It is our time, as women, to reawaken our inner genius as never before, and to bring forth our potent feminine medicine to a world seeking a way for living peacefully and honorably.

- This is a pivotal moment in history for women to be engaged in the process of changing the course of the human story.

- Together we are birthing a conscious, collaborative community of valued contributors whose diversity is seen as part of the whole. We are part of a mass awakening of the female principle within us all, where unification is the order of the day.

- Each of us is an important agent for change. Let's recognize and embrace our life encounters as divine appointments.

- We need only champion the vital part we each play, as we reach out and touch the lives of others infused with passion and purpose!

REFERENCES AND RECOMMENDATIONS

UNLEASH THE POWER OF THE FEMALE BRAIN:
Supercharging Yours for Better Health, Energy,
Mood Focus and Sex
By Daniel G. Amen

HOLODYNAMICS:
How to Develop and Manage Your Personal Power
By Vernon Wolfe

THETA HEALING:
Introducing an Extraordinary Healing Modality
By Vianna Stibil

EMOTIONAL RESILIENCE:
Simple Truths for Dealing with Unfinished Business in Your Past
By David Viscott

COSMIC CRADLE:
Souls Waiting in the Wings of Birth
By Elizabeth M. Carman and Neil J. Carmen, PhD

THE SUBTLE BODY:
An Encyclopedia of Your Energetic Anatomy
By Cyndi Dale

PRIMAL ENERGETICS:
Emotional Intelligence in Action
By Wowza

NAKED CHOCOLATE
By David Wolfe and Shazzi

REFERENCES AND RECOMMENDATIONS

IF YOU COULD HEAR WHAT I SEE:
Triumph Over Tragedy Through Laughter
By Kathy Buckley

A RETURN TO LOVE
By Marianne Williamson

THE HEALING FIRE OF HEAVEN:
Mastering the Invisible Sunlight Fluid
For Healing and Spiritual Growth
By Joseph Michael

VITAMIN D PRESCRIPTION:
The Healing Power of the Sun
By Eric Madrid

CHANGE YOUR BRAIN, CHANGE YOUR LIFE:
The Breakthrough Program for Conquering Anxiety,
Depression, Obsessiveness, Anger and Impulsiveness
By Daniel G. Amen

*We've merely
scratched the surface
when it comes to
rediscovering
how magical we,
as women, are.*

Manufactured by Amazon.ca
Bolton, ON